My Perspective
&
THOUGHTS DURING LOCKDOWN

MASARRAT AHMAD SHAH

Published By

True Dreamster Press

ISBN: 978-93-95526-15-9
MRP: Rs.249/-

Printed in India

DEDICATION

This book is dedicated to my father, a beacon of love and guidance who shaped my understanding of right and wrong. From the moment my mother departed for heaven, he selflessly prioritized my brother and me, embodying the essence of dedication and sacrifice. My father, a paragon of intellect and respect, imparted invaluable lessons on commitment and diligence in his work.

The sudden loss of loved ones to the Covid-19 pandemic, including my beloved father, was a devastating blow none of us could have anticipated. Witnessing the pain of friends who also mourned the loss of their dear ones only deepened the sense of grief and disbelief. How could we lose cherished family members to what initially seemed like an ordinary "flu"? We found ourselves grappling with the harshest realities of life, questioning why such tragedy had befallen us.

The articles and stories within these pages encapsulate my personal reflections and experiences amidst the tumultuous waves of the pandemic. Though recounting these events proved challenging, I believe that within the narrative, readers will find echoes of their own struggles and triumphs. Despite the hardships, there is solace in the shared understanding that we are not alone in our grief and that resilience can emerge from even the darkest of times.

ABOUT THE AUTHOR

Prepare to be captivated by the multi-talented force that is Masarrat Ahmad Shah. As an accomplished Author, Theatre and TV actor, Motivational speaker, and Podcaster, Masarrat possesses an unrivaled ability to capture and convey stories that truly inspire. With an unwavering dedication to exploring the intricacies of our society, He delves deep into the relationship with the world, leaving no stone unturned in the quest to shed light on human experience.

Masarrat works for IT MNC apart from his creative side. His career history demonstrates outstanding communication and leadership skills as well as a reputation for being organized and dependable.

His visionary perspective has earned him opportunities to work in global, prominent campaigns. He was engaged in Morocco with USAID and Morocco Economic University on the "Doing Business in Morocco" project. Speak on the University stage to students and inspire them for a better future.

Layered by outdoor, travel, adventure, trekking, and car enthusiast subjects, Masarrat is known for images that are punctuated by untamed, powerful landscapes.

ABOUT THE BOOK

In my second book recounting the pandemic through my lens, I delve into the events starting from December 2019, when a series of unusual pneumonia cases emerged in Wuhan, China. These cases were later identified as Coronavirus Disease 2019 (COVID-19) by the World Health Organization (WHO) on February 11, 2020. The narratives and articles within this book are drawn from my personal experiences during this tumultuous period. I aimed to encompass all the pertinent themes that characterized the time when we found ourselves confined within our homes.

During this epoch, we collectively underwent a profound transformation in our perspectives, reevaluating our perceptions of the world and the values we hold dear as individuals, as a society, and within our families. It is my belief that within the pages of this book, you will encounter events that transport you back to that time, prompting you to recognize the shared journey we all traversed. Life, with its ebbs and flows, its peaks and valleys, epitomizes the essence of our humanity, rich with a spectrum of emotions ranging from sorrow and rejection to joy and accomplishment.

I firmly maintain that an individual devoid of emotions is akin to a soul in dormancy, in need of awakening. The paradigm shift brought about by this new way of living has reintroduced us to these fundamental aspects of our existence, which we either overlooked or failed to contemplate. In our pursuit of success and competitiveness, we often neglected the simple yet profound elements of life unfolding around us.

Therefore, I invite you to immerse yourself in the pages of this book, embracing happiness regardless of circumstance, and confronting challenges with the fortitude that defines your character. It is in how we navigate through life's trials that our true essence is revealed. Trust me on this journey.

INDEX

INTRODUCTION

Life is not easy; we face a lot of challenges every day and try to fight with them to win or be successful. Who in this world had ever thought that we would see such a major shift in our lives that it would change the paradigm of our minds and the way we see things? Everyone, everyone on this globe is trying to survive. The main factor was in December 2019, a cluster of atypical cases of pneumonia was reported in Wuhan, China, which was later designated as Coronavirus disease 2019 (COVID-19) by the World Health Organization (WHO) on 11 Feb 2020. This was declared a pandemic, and worldwide, we saw lockdowns and people being locked in their dens/homes and not allowed to venture out.

We as people had lost ourselves in the hush and rush of our daily chores, whether work or anything else we were doing. The competition and being ahead of all became the utmost priority for us, we lost touch with our social set-up, families, friends, and close ones. Kids were always left alone; if they complained, their mouth was shut by giving them whatever they asked for. Our life became just like a machine running from dawn to dusk and repeating the same all the time. We lost the meaning of respect, what it means, and what we gain from it, people started worrying about themselves only and didn't care what other people think or want. The values which we had gained from our ancestors, and our parents all were falling into the cracks. Yes, one thing we all wanted is monetary gains, materialistic wins, and how one can prove to be the best.

The world is a beautiful place, and life is amazingly beautiful, but we people are stuck in our egos and false impressions. And because of this ego and bad attitude, we have fallen prey to greed, jealousy, hate, unacceptance, intolerance, and so on. We already have made our lives complex and tough with all the above areas and it makes it more complicated. Have we ever given thought to what we are doing and where are we headed, no, because we were in the rat race, with no respect for others, and no values? Now, I don't say all people are worse, there are people around us who are amazingly good, have values, give respect to others, and know what is to be done and when, however again, ignorance and ego make them drown in their not-so-good thoughts. Greed, jealousy, and ego make an animal out of them. Alas, we talk about love, compassion, brotherhood, and whatnot but no one cares about them and wants to understand them. People are caught in their thoughts which are not good, and no one can understand them, they think whatever we say is right and others are wrong, and if they do some retrospective, they will realize where they stand on their views. But as I mentioned earlier it is not easy to change the mindset of a person or an individual because they are not ready to come out of their shell, a shell of deception.

I think apart from the tragedy and havoc COVID-19 brought to the world, it also brought the realization to each of us and that was us to say HOLD, you are running too fast, take a BREAK. Honestly, this was a great relief. People were forced to stay indoors and be with their families, it was a new change and sort of challenge. Why challenge? Generally, people will be at work for 08 to 09 hours and half of their life living outside the. It became tough for everyone to stay with their families or spouses 24/7, and this also showed the cracks in the relationships and where they stand in them. Is it real or just a compromise one is doing to stay together? For some people, there were more opportunities for relaxation and fun and for others, there were some areas of improvement or challenge that required real attention. Due to COVID-19, relationships were dealing with additional stress such as job loss, reduced employment, financial hardship, and disconnection from colleagues, friends, and family which naturally have an impact on relationships. However, the lockdown taught most individuals, what relationship means and how to work on it. It brought couples together, and families together but at the same time it broke the relationships and divided the families, so there were both pros and cons to the pandemic.

There was a major impact on mental health also, with a lot of people suffering from mental issues, stress, and depression. It was not easy for people to be locked up, the same as being incarcerated in their own houses. Students, Professionals, Teachers, etc. you name it, every side of society started seeing people getting burnt out, which resulted in people committing suicide, and the situation turned out to be worse. However, some individuals tried to utilize this period bringing out new passions and talents in them. People started diverting their thoughts toward new areas, like writing, cooking, painting, and understanding the existence of the world. A new shift happened, which we called working remotely, it was a new change, everything started happening online, through Facetime, hangouts, etc., and a lot of other apps. People started working now full-time remotely, which helped organizations stay afloat without any disruption.

Friends started gathering and partying online, musicians started working on their music remotely with their musicians on screens. Everything changes dramatically in just a month. Schools, Colleges, and Universities started taking classes online. It was a new digital shift, people and organizations realized that everything could be done remotely, with no need for office spaces, etc. I will talk about it in more detail in the coming chapters. So, as I was saying about the shift in the mindset of people and bringing new individuals into them, I also turned myself to writing.

I wrote a lot of articles and stories, articles about the situation around me, stories about my real-life events, and so on. This book is a collection of my writings, and all have my perspectives on what I thought about the subject and what is my view. Surely, you will enjoy the chapters and connect yourself too in these thoughts.

Covid-19 taught us all a lot, it taught me what life means and what nature means to us. The bizarre thing that changed my view towards governments and politicians was how nature started breathing fresh air. We saw the changes in the atmosphere around us, the pollution was gone, and Mother Earth was breathing new life. Our ocean life started thriving, and to my surprise, new species of fish were discovered. People were happy to see fresh air without pollutants, we started debating about how global warming has ruined the nature and natural habitat on this planet. This was again a new lesson for us from Mother Nature to make us think. Think about what is important and what is not necessary, and how can we reduce the things that we use to affect and pollute the planet, oceans, mountains, rivers, and whatnot.

So, let us get started with all my thoughts and my perspectives in further chapters.

Chapter 1- Searching for Solitude

The essence of human connection, respect, and empathy seems to have slipped away from us. We no longer distinguish between empathy and sympathy as we once did. Sadly, we have bid farewell to the precious times when a simple "Hello" or "Hey" and a genuine smile conveyed understanding and warmth, rather than the impersonal "Smiley" emojis of today.

We must acknowledge the growing number of individuals seeking refuge from cities, towns, and even social responsibilities in pursuit of salvation and solitude. Why is this happening? Do you have any insights or explanations to share?

Recently, I watched a program on #BBC Earth, "Where the Wild Men are with #Ben Fogle", I was surprised to see how established well to do and well-settled people have left their world life and live in some remote jungles and islands, happily and without any disturbance, from people around or social media. People are going back to the Old Age style of living, where they breed cattle, grow their vegetables, and do a little bit of farming for their survival. Watched a film on Ian Usher, who was doing very well in his career and living happily in Australia, but because of stress and a disturbing marriage that turned into Divorce, he auctioned his entire life – car, home, job, and friends – on eBay in a midlife crisis that made headlines the world over. He owns a Caribbean Island now and is living happily. And like him, there are so many more people.

Why are we running from everything around us, what is bothering us? Nowadays, we have everything available at our fingertips, isn't it? I have an answer, the reason is we don't have #**PEACE**. We all are searching for peace and tranquility which has gone from none to never. Technology is giving us so many things every day, be it IoT, AI, machine learning, Robots, and so on. Social media is killing us all, WhatsApp, FB, Twitter, Instagram, and so on. We have lost our privacy rights. We are growing in Artificial Technology, resulting in the emergence of Robots and the Loss of humans. Soon, we will see only Robots around and Humans will be here and there, as they will be running towards the stone age.

So, I am wondering if we are heading to disaster and the end of this human race as we have started building Robots and machines with human intelligence and ending the living people or pushing them to get out, saying, if you want to survive to go back to the stone age as you don't fit here. Experts all over the work have predicted that networked artificial intelligence will amplify human effectiveness but also threaten human autonomy, agency, intellect, and capabilities. They expressed a wide range of possibilities; that computers might match or even exceed human intelligence and capabilities on tasks such as complex decision-making, reasoning and learning, sophisticated analytics and pattern recognition, visual acuity, speech recognition, and language translation. As they said "smart", systems in communities, in vehicles, in buildings and utilities, on farms, and in business processes will save time, money, and lives and offer opportunities for individuals to enjoy a more-customized future. And we are seeing driverless cars, trucks, and state of art robots in manufacturing plants doing amazing jobs. So, where do humans, the people, and individual workers go and do? This is where people are getting fear of how to survive without work or a job, and how will they feed their kids. The world is getting tougher and more competitive with the emergence of technology. This is one of the reasons people are running away from materialistic life and embracing lonely life of peace and being themselves.

Can we all put ON thinking Caps and try to analyze where is the balance and where should we draw a line?

We all are humans with flesh and blood, and we need human touch, we cannot live in the virtual world and be friends or well-wishers on just social media. We are losing our health, minds, respect for others, and most importantly ourselves because of this technology boom. I am not against technology; it has done wonderful things, but we need to have a place for everything. Take the relationships, under Covid-19 lockdowns, people realized what relationship means to them in a real way, are they really into one another, or are they just fulfilling the compromise they have agreed on?

A lot of arguments and fights and blame games started emerging among couples, and partners. Once I saw a Facebook video where in some village in India, a husband was arguing with his wife and they were fighting in a lane where all neighbors were looking and seeing what was going on, but no one was coming to stop them and tell them enough just stop, but none and to my shock, the husband took out a pistol from his pocket and shit his wife at point blank. I think she may have died then and there. This is what lockdowns did to married couples as they were not used to living and being in front of each other 24/7, night and day many families did enjoy spending more time together during the pandemic, but some relationships failed to thrive during a period of unprecedented upheavals and uncertainties as I mentioned above. The COVID-19 pandemic took an immense emotional toll on mankind, with people around the world dealing with the tragic loss of loved ones and heightened everyday pressures that have come from living, working, and schooling from home.

The divorce rate increased during the pandemic — the U.K.'s largest family law firm reported a 95% increase in divorce inquiries during the pandemic (with women driving the surge in interest). While in the U.S., Legal Templates, which sells legal forms written by licensed attorneys, reported a 34% increase in sales of its divorce agreement in the first half of 2020 (when the lockdown kicked in), so, seeing these statistics, it is obvious that people started running away from the courtships and relationships to be alone and live in peace. Children are suffering a lot because of this running away from relationships and embracing aloofness. When a kid is seeing his/her parents separating because of arguments, stress, and undue demands they are shattered. The danger of this is a new generation growing up with mental health issues and chaotic childhood, so how will we accept them to understand relationships, emotional needs, etc, they will be forced to live a lonely, miserable life and of course, will run for Solitude.

We need to understand and realize it soon, rather than at the point where it's too late and nothing can be done to fix it. We need to think about our future generations and make sure they have a real understanding of emotional bonds and relationships. They should respect one another rather than cutthroat toward each other. Finding solitude and solace is good and it does remunerate a person or an individual, however, this should not be at the cost of failed relationships, emotional distress, and mental health issues because of loss of job, loved ones, and a life they want to live.

"The best thinking has been done in solitude. The worst has been done in turmoil." – Thomas A. Edison

Chapter 2- What if we are going to Die Tomorrow?

One thing is sure what we learned from the coronavirus pandemic is, that life is short, and no one knows when we will be breathing our last breath. We all know life is unpredictable and death is inexorable, but it will show us so soon, honestly, we never expected it. In the various waves of covid, around there have been 6, 407, 556 deaths reported by WHO. So, many died can you imagine, it's a catastrophe and no one in this world was prepared for this be it Governments, health systems, or people. Our health system failed to handle this pandemic. Today, the person is good with his/her family trying to keep safe, and the next moment within days that person is dead, leaving families shell-shocked and shattered. People lost hope, hope to live, and see the world again as it was before the pandemic.

Well, we all were so busy with our daily lives and our busy routines, and we forgot about things around us, or we didn't care about what was going on around us or in our society. All were running for their bit and making sure that whatever is their job, we do that better and on top of that make sure no one else goes ahead, which we call Competition and I say Rat Race.

How many of us think about, what if I were not alive tomorrow or what if I faced sudden death as we saw in the pandemic, we all may have seen or heard of such instances, I have heard and even lost my friends. Today he is with me at work, and we are sipping coffee, chatting in the cafeteria, giggling, and cracking jokes, and the next day he is no more, sudden death and a total shock for all friends, family, and colleagues. What happened, did that person know he was about to die, or his/her time was over, no he/she didn't, nor did we know, moreover we don't want to know. All of us are occupied with thoughts of investments, jobs, hikes, growth, vacations, just planning and planning and planning and no idea about the end, a closure of mind and heart, loss of soul in the void and our spirit which will be hanging somewhere in skies between Heaven and Hell, and to tell you about this, there are various stories where the Spirit will go after leaving one's body.

Why am I writing about death, why did this thought come to me, and what made me start thinking about this subject? The only, reason is me seeing people leaving us or going to leave us anytime. Can I ask you a question, how many times a day do you think about death? Do we? No, we don't, we should because we don't know when we are going to breathe our last breath. What if we knew when we were going to die, have you ever thought or imagined, say, we would have been made aware at the time of birth or any stage of our life that, here is your date of death with time and place? What will you do then, stop living, stop caring about others or yourself, stop caring or thinking about things which I discussed earlier, job, etc.? Or will we start, living more, give our best to the people around us, and be more caring and loving? Forget about caste, creed, or religion, stop being racist, love all, and be more understanding, and respectful towards family, people, community, society, and friends. One will be a more motivated individual to spend the best of time in this limited time on Earth. Because there will be respect for that period that person is here and must accomplish as many good deeds as one can and make the best out of that limited period.

Do you know what some of those changes look like? When reminded of death, we treat those who are like us in looks, political slant, geographic origin, and religious beliefs more favorably. We will become more contemptuous towards people who do not share those similarities. We will profess a deeper commitment to romantic partners who validate our worldviews, and we tend to be calmer and more spiritual and peaceful.

The reverse can also happen we can become more careless, anarchic, start drinking, smoking, eating whatever we want, and so on because we don't care now. Society will change, norms will change, and how people think about religion and other areas will change. There will be a new way of living in this world, people will not worry about governments or Politicians or who is doing what. But, yes the way rules and policies are currently will change definitely. People who will run the societies will have new rules to discipline the people. Does the understanding that our final breath could come tomorrow affect the way we choose to live? And how do we make sense of a life cut short by any sudden event, say an accident or cardiac arrest, which is very common? Death is all around us every day, as per Islam, death is always walking with you at your back and can suddenly come in front of you. When it can come no one knows, which is what we are talking about what if we know when this angel of death will suddenly appear and say "Hello, your time is up". Now, both in politics and in everyday life, one of the worst things we could do is get used to death and treat it as unremarkable or as anything other than a loss. This fact has profound consequences for every facet of life: politics and governance, interpersonal relationships, and all forms of human consciousness. When things go well, you are doing your best in life and there is nothing to worry about, death stays in the background, and from there, covertly, it shapes our awareness of everything else. However, even when we get through the day with ease, the prospect of death is still in some way all around us which we do not realize or don't think about.

The philosophers Soren Kierkegaard and Martin Heidegger each have discussed death, in their ways, as a horizon that implicitly shapes our consciousness. It's what gives future times the pressure they exert on us. A horizon is a kind of thing that is normally in the background — something that limits, partly defines, and sets the stage for what you focus on. These two philosophers help us see the ways that death occupies the background of consciousness — and that the background is where it belongs.

Death is standing. It's standing in the way liquid stands still in a container. Start, thinking and remembering about death every day and say " I do remember you". What if nothing is with us tomorrow? Stop hating each other and pulling each other down at work, in the political system, at your office, and around your society. Be a humble, calm, and peace-loving individual, give your best at any side of your life or any job you are doing, and be honest and transparent. We are not on this Earth forever, no one is. So, why do we need unhealthy competition, racism, corruption, religious divides, and communalism? Why all these negative things, for what? Stop spreading hate on social media and spreading fake news. Use social media for spreading Peace, Love, and Harmony. Discuss positive things, and good stuff and motivate others to live in the happiest possible way.

"A brush with death always helps us to live our lives better." - Paulo Coelho

Chapter 3- Where is the Humanity?

As per wise learned people "Humanity" means the human race, which includes everyone on Earth, mind you I am stressing here on EVERYONE ON EARTH and there is a reason for it.

The word humanity is from the Latin humitas for "human nature, kindness." Humanity includes all humans, but it can also refer to the kind feelings humans often have for each other. Awww, wow really, how many people know about these feelings, I am searching for these adjectives around.

Sometimes I keep thinking and trying to understand what we humans have turned into, and the word that comes to my mind is guess what "Vultures". Everyone is constantly in search of prey and pound on it and finish off to declare victory or superiority over others. Where are we learning from all these tricks and trades of being predators and what is making us do that? I am not pointing out any individual or section or community, we all are, so-called 21st Century mankind doing this or involved in this game, in some, or the other way. New sections are emerging every day that are trying to make their point for their survival as they feel threatened to be part of the society or community. And we know the phrase "Survival of the Fittest", and that is true to some extent, in terms of competition, business, political games, etc. But not in terms of Bias, Racism, Caste, Religion, etc.

There are new terms in the whole world, and these are emerging in every corner, Right Wing, Left Wing, Centre Wing, etc. Why? What are these sections trying to prove that one is superior to the other or that only one Wing will rule this World and other Wings are not allowed and will perish or be wiped off? Why? Who is inducing these thoughts in people and making them believe that you belong to this wing and not the other? Why are people threatening that if you don't comply or agree to one Wing you will be wiped off? Who decides that, and what is the purpose, isn't this an insecurity that is creeping into everyone's mind? As they feel insecure and threatened, they try to do all types of destruction to prove their stand so that no one takes them for granted.

If an individual, community, or section of people feel Insecure or Threatened, it's obvious they take the route which is extreme and violent to prove their existence because they are forced to do that. In an earlier time when there were big empires and dynasties, and King used to be brutal and threaten people, people revolted and become violent, same is happening now, our Governments and Political System is turning into Empires and Kings, they want to rule with force, draconian laws, my way or highway, Democracy is dead, and it is just now a Word used which does not have meaning. Because of this, we are seeing the change in how these people rule us and the result is various Wings to stop others from Rule. Because it's either Right or Left or Centre Wing section who wants to Rule us.

Please stop all this mess, our earth is already under tremendous stress and it's obvious because we have Global Warming, which is winning all games, every part of the earth is almost destroyed, the environment is in shambles and if one raises the voice they are threatening to shut up. And the latest is Mr. Covid-19, this Virus realized why should I be left out, let me wipe off these people who have messed up the whole earth and are responsible for everything. And we are calling it Pandemic and fighting it fighting a Silent War from each corner of the World, none is spared. Bravo, this is what we deserve because everyone still is busy with their Image and how they can Rule each other and prove their Superiority

You know, today I am creating a new Wing and I belong to it and will never move out of it because I also need to survive and help others to survive too, and I call this wing "Humanity Wing". Yes, it's better we realize soon that we are humans and if we are sent to this Earth by Almighty, then there is a reason, maybe to take of each other, take care of Animals, Jungles, Oceans and keep this beautiful earth as it was given to us. We must stop thinking of being biased toward each other, stop creating these sections and communities, and work as one under Humanity Wing. We all are the same, and all have the right to live and enjoy this earth. Not only Black Lives Matter or White Lives Matter, or this Live matter and not the other, All Lives Matter to LIVE. We need to build a System of technology Artificial Intelligence etc, to understand Humanity and treat everyone the same.

We all have Blood in our veins which is RED, do Black have a different color than white, or do Americans have a different color than Indians or Africans? Do we have any difference in our Anatomy, I don't have an extra Eye or Nose than yours, is it and yes you will be laughing but it's true we think like that. We all are humans first than any other individual belonging to one section of the community or belonging to one religion. We all must Respect and Understand each other, I think we need new courses in our schools and colleges which will stop teaching them to divide one from another and make them understand we all are one as humans and Humanity come first.

Human unity is the recent interpretation of humanity, where we need to have unity in thought processes & actions like empathizing with not only our human race but also with all the species of our planet Earth. Well said that we need only one wing which is the Human Wing. When would a human realize and change his/her thoughts and actions? One way out is to have thoughts in-school sessions, about Humanity in all the learning phases like schools, colleges, universities, etc. It shall be nurtured right from the stage for children as tiny tots till they graduate themselves or at least the tenth grade in the suburban areas. Let us know, remember that human is just one among the millions of species on earth. Then why does he manage things? We must be able to live as a true human being. Like charity begins from home, humanity begins from our hearts. Like anything else, in our work, and studies, we need to "own" our 'humanness' to sheer away the vulture culture.

As I mentioned at the start Humanity belongs to everyone and it means to show kindness, respect, and compassion towards each entity on this earth. If I respect you then only you will respect me, and so on. We cannot forget this concept of living; this is the fundamental discipline of life. Our Politicians and Individuals who choose to run the state or Governments need to understand this theory and apply it and they will be successful and will beat every enemy like Covid-19 and people will be safe and live without fear. We need Peace and Tranquility; we don't need Hatred and Destruction.

As the child grows, he's fed so many things into his system which grasps everything super-fast. The surrounding, the environment where the child is growing up, the issues, the famine, the fights, the arguments, the hatred, etc., so many negatives fed right straight into his system. Most of them grow up with a mindset that's been taught and seen. Very few reasons for all of it and cone out of it. Hence the majority will fall into one of the wings as you mentioned above. I personally also feel 'that religion' is one of the major factors leading to wars amongst people. A child should never be fed religion, let him/her choose if they require knowing what they want to believe in.

I conclude by saying this, if we love each other regardless of who they are, living in peace and harmony is not so far from reality. Our Children need to live freely and enjoy themselves rather than getting killed and orphaned because of our hatred for each other. Please do not spoil their minds and thoughts, do not corrupt them with these divisions of "Wings" and teach them about only one Wing which is HUMANITY WING.

"You must not lose faith in Humanity. Humanity is an ocean; if a few drops of the ocean are dirty, the ocean does not become dirty." – Mahatma Gandhi

Chapter 4- Capitalism, Covid-19, and Catastrophe

Was this Virus created or was it an accident? The latest revelation by researchers and scientists who were still trying to find the origin of this virus concluded that it originated from the Wuhan fish market. Anyways, why did suddenly in 2020 the whole world come to a grinding halt? Why was China blamed or was China part of this Game, who all are partners in this disaster, and who benefited from this Pandemic? Why rich get richer and the poor/middle-class down to just hand to mouth situation and now from poor to poorer?

I am sure you have heard about the word Capitalism, yes right, it is the economic system in which businesses are owned and run for profit by individuals and not by the state. Few say 1% of the powerful business houses run the whole system and make sure that their interests are safe, and nothing affects them. These are the people who for their beneficial interests disrupt the system Globally, I am sure you remember the financial meltdown of 2007.

The COVID-19 pandemic has exposed multiple structural flaws of global capitalism in every nook and corner of the world. These have been reproduced through the intensification of inequalities and reinforced through policy responses that have failed to protect the most vulnerable from the health and socio-economic impacts of COVID-19. The COVID-19 pandemic has also revealed the materiality of human activity and complex geographies of inequality whether it is America, Europe, or any other country and the worst has been seen in developing countries like Africa, South Asia, etc. Working population, small businesses poor families have been most affected. People have lost their jobs and businesses. But the Richer is not seeing the brunt of this and they are working on making more and more profits, like pharmaceutical companies, E-Commerce giants, etc.

The COVID-19 crisis is exposing more and more flaws in our economic structures, not least the increasing precarity of work, owing to the rise of the gig economy and a decades-long deterioration of workers' bargaining power. Telecommuting simply is not an option for most workers, and although governments are extending some assistance to workers with regular contracts, the self-employed may find themselves left high and dry. The insurance companies are minting money like crazy taking advantage of vulnerable people and putting them into debt for a lifetime.

We are seeing a lot of philanthropists coming forward and donating millions and millions of their wealth for Food, Medicine, Research, and so on, but do you know why they are doing this? They are giving something to gain back more of it from Governments and People. If a billion dollars is invested in the vaccine industry, in return they are asking for a double after it is deployed to the public. The prices of everything are so high, it has tripled. The Hand sanitizer or Mask which none of the people used to use, now have to buy it and the price is not less than 20-25$ where it was just for a dollar or two and lying on the shelf. So, again who is making money?

In the New York Times "Neil Irwin" wrote in 2020, that Pfizer had reached a $1.95 billion "advance purchase" agreement with the United States government, ensuring it would be well compensated for eventually delivering 100 million doses of vaccine. In other words, though the government did not directly fund the drug development, it created the groundwork in which the pharmaceutical company could spend research dollars with abandon, knowing that success would be financially rewarded. The Pandemic Is Showing Us How Capitalism Is Amazing and Inadequate. There was research completed on Vaccines for the Sars virus in 2018 which would have cured Coronavirus also, but the big pharma companies denied producing vaccines because they thought it is not worth profits and instead of developed drugs worth profits like Viagra.

Take any country only Billionaires are adding more zeros to their wealth and exploring Space, and some are denying people the right to live or have their say on their Produce, such as Farmers. And Middle class and working class are dying of hunger and uncertainty. Why are we not seeing these richest tycoons dying and suffering from covid, why are only the Middle and Work sections of the population getting buried in thousands, and why are these people only losing their loved ones? Who took their right to Live and Breathe?

So, the Governments and Business Giants are hands in hand with this Catastrophic Pandemic. They are just worried about their Wealth, Position, and Power. People are not important to them, they are just mere workers who work for them and are surviving on their mercy. Societies are in shambles; people are crying for mercy and help but no one is coming forward and listening to them. Take on-going wars in various countries, why is that again Capitalism, how will these big ammunition and war-building companies survive if they can't sell their advanced destructive products? So, the countries are inducing these wars and letting people die and perish, and the State Heads and Business Tycoons are laughing and having a good time because they are making Billions from these atrocities

Rightly said by Mariana Mazzucato, the writer is a professor at University College London, If there is an economic lesson from the past 12 months, it is this: Covid-19 is the moment to do capitalism differently. The pandemic showed our economic system is not simply in crisis, it is structurally flawed.

Many times, people think and know the reason for the outbreak of the Coronavirus, but none want to come out boldly to submit the facts. You have exposed the stark-naked truth about the ongoing Covid crisis. In the beginning, there was so much hype telling the kind that we humans learned big lessons. But what happened was that people learned to be not noble but notorious criminals amidst the chaos suffered by the middle classes and lower classes of society exploitation of all kinds the paved way to make humans mean and undervalued guinea pigs for the richer and powerful people. People who made hay while the sun shined like those who made masks, sanitizers, gloves, PPE Kits, etc made themselves billionaires. The rest of the people don't, one after another in the second wave of the Covid crisis. Who won? something that is the meaning of humanity? It lost its meaning in totality. It's a world of warcraft in the disguise of biological weapons to become Capitalists.

Reflecting on our school days when we studied the history of the two world wars, there was often speculation about the possibility of a third world war. Considering the current global situation, one might argue that what we are experiencing is indeed akin to a third world war. Everyone seems to have been enlisted as soldiers in a biological battle, struggling for oxygen and access to life-saving medications. Countless individuals have lost their loved ones, their life savings, and many have been left orphaned by the devastating consequences of this ongoing crisis.

This is the war by the powerful allies on the earth money-making by the Governments and Pharmaceutical industry. No doubts about it. Ashoka the great king repented seeing the blood making the battlefield completely red. He could not bear seeing his brethren fallen dead. There was reconciliation during King Ashoka's regime in the land of Kalinga. The same reconciliation will never happen now. If Ashoka the great were created during the pandemic, we would have had a better world to live in! It is Surely, people will live with the challenge on their own as we must help ourselves. But it is otherwise for the majority the humans. Why say that devils reside in hell? Devils reside in between us, within our society.

So, in the end, what I say is we need to think differently, businesses need to work on a structural way of making thin thatch that will help people and society rather than just a few business groups. 1% of Billionaires of this world have half the amount of wealth globally while the rest of the Globe is poor and struggling to survive. We now need a better Society, Equality, Peace, and Tranquility. And all this in place we a be a better world.

The question is, is that Possible?

"Nothing should be more obvious than that the business organism cannot function according to design when its most important 'parameters of action'—wages, prices, interest—are transferred to the political sphere and there dealt with according to the requirements of the political game or, which sometimes is more serious still, according to the ideas of some planners." - Joseph A. Schumpeter

Chapter 5- New Buzz, Great Resignations

The new buzz started in 2021 and all over media there were related to "Great Resignations", people leaving their jobs for good, and yes, it's not they are opting for other work areas. People burnt out and stressed because of working from home with loads of pressure from management to meet deadlines also, there was one more theory company forcing employees to join offices back which was not acceptable to employees as they had invested in home offices and also were worried about their safety and health.

Why are people leaving jobs, work as we all know is an important factor which pays our bills, feeds our family, and is a way of survival and satisfaction. But, since pandemics struck our lives and changed the whole spectrum of the Globe, people started adapting to new ways of life, working, and adjusting to unexpected changes. As an employee, I always wanted to work from home for a day or two and it was a luxury if your company provides this sort of benefit, and yes, I had that luxury, thanks to my organization and the management to allow us to work from home if required. It was a privilege but at the same time, there were disadvantages also, like missing the meetings at work, brainstorming on projects with the teams, etc.

No one knew that this will be our new norm, working from home for good. People in the initial months enjoyed it and started adjusting to it, work was running smooth, with no hiccups all giving their best to make sure delivery and organization goals are not affected. Employees became more and more productive, companies recognized that the productivity of employees has increased drastically. Home offices started flourishing people started setting up their small workplaces and companies supported this too as all-new, we are not going to be back to the workplace in the coming time.

But what happened after a year of the Pandemic and continue working from home and giving more than 100% of productivity? Did management start recognizing the time and effort employees are putting IN and making the business flourish and gain profits, I will say not really,.No? People started feeling fatigued and got burnt out, it does not only work they are handling from home, there are other priorities also, Kids, Parents, House Chores, etc. everything has piled up and it must be done. This huge workload piling up and on top of that Covid-19 created a mess all around, taking our friends, and loved ones made people vulnerable. People started getting into depression and anxiety increased, resulting in fights, divorces, and suicides. What a mess, utter chaos.

Then suddenly companies decided to get employees back to office space as pre-pandemic time, of course not 100% presence but as 20% to 30%. Now, companies have started adopting the Hybrid model, where an employee can come to the office twice a week and work remotely on rest days. This also created a panic among workers and employees as all of them had adopted to work from home offices, invested in the home offices and besides that moved to their native places where they had come from to cities and new places where their companies were. Employees were not ready to break that norm now as they were comfortable, working and also spending time with their loved ones where they were away earlier and visiting their families once a year or so. This also triggered mass resignations as people were not ready to jeopardize their health and safety.

Coming back to our topic, the whole unexpected chaotic circumstances made people think, about what they wanted. Do they want to continue like this and end up in the Grave or take a leap off this hush and rush and Live? Companies are not recognizing the sacrifices employees are making, they just hear them in office meetings and make sure work is done. According to the U.S. Bureau of Labor Statistics, 4 million Americans quit their jobs in July 2021. Resignations peaked in April and have remained abnormally high for the last several months, with a record-breaking 10.9 million open jobs at the end of July. How can employers retain people in the face of this tidal wave of resignations?

Employers Must Take a Data-Driven Approach to Improve Retention, these trends highlight the importance of taking a data-driven approach to determining not just how many people are quitting, but who exactly has the highest turnover risk, why people are leaving, and what can be done to prevent it. The details will look different in every organization, but three steps can help any employer more effectively leverage data to improve employee retention:

1. Find the root cause of the issue, why are employees leaving, and how can we retain them. Having a retention

policy is a must in this present scenario. The employer needs to recognize the efforts employees are putting IN and make the work not get affected.

2. Empathize with employees, management and HR must play a big role here. Just having virtual meditation sessions and talks will not work. Managers must see what an employee is going through and does he/she require help or support.

3. Reward and recognize the hard work and efforts employees are putting IN, appreciate the work they are doing, and say thanks to them. Employees are the priority and more important than your customer. If they, leave your work gets affected and organizations are losing top talent and a loyal workforce.

4. Once you have identified the root cause, and why employees are putting down papers, you can begin to create highly customized programs aimed at correcting the specific issues that your workplace struggles with most. One higher-level intervention that may be necessary before you can begin any sort of targeted campaign is to invest in an organized, user-friendly system for tracking and analyzing the metrics that will inform your retention efforts.

5. Companies need to adapt to the Hybrid Model, let employees decide when they want to come into the office, and give them a choice to choose the days in a week to be in the office. Covid-19 taught us new ways of living and working, so we need to adopt the new change and yes, like this we will see satisfied employees and an increase in productivity.

So, with greater visibility into both how serious your turnover problem is, and the root causes that drive it, you'll be empowered to attract top talent, reduce turnover costs, and ultimately build a more engaged and effective workforce. It will be a win-win situation for both Employee and Employer. Companies focus on retaining people and guiding them in these difficult times. Managers need to lead the way and take more responsibility and onus for making sure no one is left behind, empathize, and recognize.

"Don't judge each day by the harvest you reap but by the seeds that you plant." –

Chapter 6- Shut-Up – Self Censorship

Instead of engaging in futile debates, fruitless discussions, toxic arguments, and meaningless trolling, I have chosen to remain silent and withhold my words.

A few days back I was watching a program on Al-Jazeera "B-Studio Unscripted" where intellectual minds come and talk on issues, society, arts, etc., and was listening to one of the great artists Anish Kapoor, he was mentioning how art is more like a rebellion or as Picasso had once said "Art is a War" and talking about the impact of art and artist on the society on whole. He used the word self-censorship. I was intrigued by this word and concept, and immediately my thoughts started running, thinking yes, he is right why should we not just keep ourselves quiet rather than be involved in senseless social media trolls and fake information? And if this censorship is applied, a lot of issues will automatically be solved.

We are living in utter chaos, surrounded by fake news, fabricated issues, biased views, and what not, we all know very well somewhere in our hearts and sub-conscious that all this is not real, this mess and chaos are creating more uncertainty and divisions in our society, democracy, and social fabric. You know, in the US elections there were close to 140 fake news websites identified where the source of data was mostly Facebook. As per Craig Silverman, media editor of Buzzfeed, in mid-2016, a funny stream of completely made-up stories seemed to originate from one small eastern European town. "We ended up finding a small cluster of news websites all registered in the same town in Macedonia called Velves, Silverman recalls, as per BBC reporting.

Why we need to just keep away from this fake news, is because they are not only a threat to democracies but us as people. This fake news is relentlessly targeting hyper-partisan views, which play to the fears and prejudices of people to influence their voting patterns and their behavior. We have seen this not only in USA the elections but in other countries too, like India, and latest in France. So, what is the impact of this fake news or information, Twitter feeds and trolls, and main media news, and yes, WhatsApp universities, it's changing and distorting how political campaigns are run, and yes the legitimacy of these elections, elected officials and governments are Questionable.

Several well-publicized incidents have demonstrated the negative impact of false information. As an example, early during the pandemic, questions were raised regarding the possible use of disinfectants administered internally to patients with COVID-19. Misinformation further aggravates an already complex emotional situation. Healthcare providers are not immune to these effects. A recent study evaluated the mental health effects of COVID-19 in healthcare workers. Over 70% reported psychological distress, with symptoms including anxiety, depression, and insomnia. These traumatic emotional effects are heightened by conflict, confusion, and conspiracy theories circulating in the news media and online. Doctors, Nurses were just battling with the patients, their trauma, and with that their heightened stress which they were unable to express in front of the patients. Some doctors even posted the personal trauma they are going through on their social posts.

Hundreds of fake posts related to CoVID-19 are posted online on FB, Twitter, WhatsApp, etc, people are saying not to take vaccines because no one knows what is in them, but at the same time, they don't try to understand the pain and agony of those who lost their loved ones to this virus. When someone lost their loved one due to COVID1-19 then they realized "Oh, it's fatal" We must be careful and decide for ourselves what is wrong and what is not, do our research and think rather than blindly accepting these fake and unknown facts and posts.

Now, how can we as the People of our Country and as part of our society clear our thoughts and mind from getting corrupted by these toxic 24/7 feeds which are untrue and fabricated? The only way is to "SHUT-UP" and yes, "SELF-CENSOR" yourself. We need to stop getting sucked or tangled in unethical, biased, racist topics and discussions. Get away from News Channels of any kind, they are spreading one-sided story which is without facts and are biased. They are controlling your mind continuously by feeding junk like venom. It's human nature, if you feed your brain or mind something repeatedly then you will be affected, it is like hypnotism, we are being hypnotized every second. And people who do not understand and ignore real issues, except their views without questioning, start believing all their nonsense crap and in turn poison others around them, friends, family, and yes society because somewhere we all are vulnerable.

From my perspective, one should think before acting or making any decision. I know we all are not the same illogical, irrational stupid; we know what is going on, and whom all are going to gain from this. Are they rewarding you to form their success, giving you positions, money, etc, "NO" and will never give you, we are pawns in their hand? Say something happens or we are under attack, we people will be on the front line or the firing line, see what is happening in Ukraine, who is dying in streets like dogs, the common man and the Army person personnel any government official or Mayor or minister died, No, these politicians and bureaucrats are involved in the "Game of Sanctions"?

Finally, my request to all who are reading this, stop being biased, Irrational, and Fake, think before you take or decide on saying agree or disagree, or most importantly post anything on social media. Use your intelligence, think logically, and see if it makes any sense, who will gain from it, and who will lose. In the end, be real people with rational thinking, stop getting into cults or wings, and Be You.

"The mind is not a vessel to be filled but a fire to be kindled." - Plutarch

Chapter 7- Suicide, Death of a Soul

Well, I am tired of this world, the people, and society. Everyone has their own opinion and prejudices where they are not ready to accept me or listen to me or say understand me. Why should I live here, where no one is bothered about me being here or not?

Every day we hear stories about Suicide, on news channels, in newspapers, and on social media, and to my surprise, we have seen people committing this extreme act LIVE on Facebook. I wonder what makes them do it, what is going through their mind at the time when they are making themselves, their body, and their soul go through such a painful act or process. Do they listen to themselves, or do they pause for a moment and rethink the consequences after this step is completed, am I hurting someone by making them part of this pain?

Saying goodbye to the people and feeling the pain and agony of leaving them, have anyone thought Why? But yes, we hear the news and for a few minutes we express sadness and empathy with that individual, and in a second thought, we curse him/her. We start judging, saying how cowardly act he/she did, a loser not able to handle the situation, rather than facing the consequences, the person took an easier way to run away from the issues and life and left his loved ones to suffer. Well, most of the people say, why was not help asked, like psychiatrist, counselor. But my question is who is responsible for this act of what you call cowardliness or being looser, who should we blame, is this blame going to only that individual who suffered so much and said enough is enough? Who made him think that and act on it? Why was not anyone there to listen and care and guide? Was there anyone to empathize with, forget about sympathy. And I am sure the answer is "NO". What we, as people or society do, is talk, talk, and talk and pass comments and make judgments. We are so inhuman that we don't even care to think before we say it.

If a person is happy and content with his or her life, why will there be a question or thought of ending life? But what happens is when an individual goes through hell because of another person then the issues arise. Everyone is stressed, angry, irritated, and displeased with various issues in life. Whether it is a relationship, parents, employee-manager relationship, marriage problems, and so on. There is chaos because of some disconnect, misunderstanding, and miscommunication between two individuals. We are seeing everyday fights, abuses, and what not happening in homes, offices, and workplaces. People are being Judged, Racist, biased, Cast attacks, and whatnot. Some people handle it to some extent but at one point they lose it and when they start hating everything and when that brim of patience passes, they either think to finish themselves or that person who is the reason for the whole mess. So, there is a trigger point, someone is taking that individual to that edge where the extreme step takes the place of either Murder or Suicide, where I believe both are "Murders".

So, who is responsible for this Murder in either case? Not that person but we as a society are responsible for a person to take such a heinous and extreme step. As a society, we are murdering that person, where we say suicide was committed. Yes, we see and have seen and heard enough suicide notes where the deceased had mentioned, "for my death no one is responsible, I am myself responsible for taking my own life", why does that person say that because he knows that there is no hope, whom all will they punish where the whole society is responsible for this crime, for this murder of me. He/she is done with society and the fake empathy and kindness of people who were "Loved Ones".

We all are hypocrites, running from reality and living in some fantasy world. Seeing movies and the glamorous life in reel life, we feel that's the life we want and try to copy and live. But sorry friends that's not the way we live, understand the real world. We all need respect, love, and compassion. Our society and world need peace and tranquility where all live equally and there is no racism, bias, or prejudice. Because of our inhumane attitude and losing ourselves in the virtual, social media, and AI world we are losing our loved ones, our friends, and our dear ones. Stop this madness and love each other, talk to each other, show care and compassion, and sort things out rather than fight over things. Everyone has trouble, issues, and disagreements but they can be resolved and worked out if and only if we show real consciousness and compassion. Suicide is not a Solution; it is an easy way to end the misery of life.

Well, yes, I want to live and be happy see the world and be a successful person. Yes, I want to love and be loved with real passion and zeal. But don't judge me, misunderstand me, and leave me to myself. Please listen to me and try to talk to me, maybe we will find a solution, which will support me to prove myself and be a better human being, a better person, and make this world a better and peaceful place. Show me some respect and you will get an abundance of responses. Lastly, I know suicide is a crime, a sin, a very ugly and heinous sin, and I don't want to take that step but be there for me when I need it and help me to understand rather than throwing me in my depressed hole where I have no one to listen and talk.

"The purpose of our lives is to be happy." — Dalai Lama.

Chapter 8- Police, Prison, and the Prisoner

When a child is born, no one knows what lies in the future or the fate of this baby. The baby is just like an angel born with just a cry and smile. The glimpse of the baby is so adorable that one does not want to stop loving him/her.

When this child starts growing, how its mindset and future will be carved depends on the parents the baby was born to and the society and culture he/she grows. The most important part is the socio-economic background of this child which will define and design their future for him. No one is born CEO or President, or Thief or Murderer and we all know it. It all depends on the education that this child receives and the family values and ethics which are imparted by the Parents and the Society.

There are instances, where having everything around can still change the fate of the person. The person can become or change their stance as per the circumstances and the situation he is facing. Say, for example, an individual wants to be an Engineer but because of competition, family pressure, or peer pressure, he/she chooses a profession other the Engineering. Take one more example. All is going well with Mr.Z and suddenly he sees the opportunity to make tons of money by doing a little bit of fraud here and there and gets corrupted. Mr.Y is performing well in his career and suddenly gets caught in a conspiracy that he never was part of, but because he was at the wrong place at the wrong time gets caught and ends up in Jail for a crime which he was not aware off and is now called criminal.

So, what I am saying is all the people who end up in jails, do we try to think as to why they ended up there, what could have been the reason for their fate that made them take drastic steps, or were they involved in crimes that turned them into a criminal.

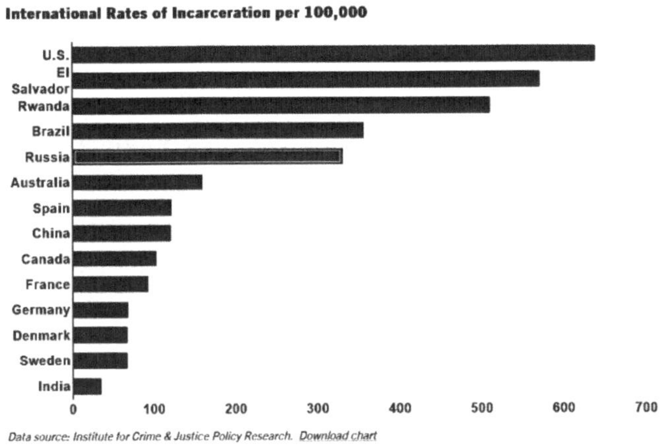

According to sentencingproject.org, There are 2 million people in the United States prisons and jails—a 500% increase over the last 40 years. There are changes in sentencing law and policy, but no changes in crime rates, explain most of this increase. These trends have resulted in prison overcrowding and fiscal burdens on states to accommodate a rapidly expanding penal system, despite increasing evidence that large-scale incarceration is not an effective means of achieving public safety.

More people were sent to prisons, and sentencing policies of the War on Drugs era resulted in dramatic growth in incarceration for drug offenses. Since its official beginning in the 1980s, the number of Americans incarcerated for drug offenses has skyrocketed from 40,900 in 1980 to 430,926 in 2019. Furthermore, harsh sentencing laws such as mandatory minimums keep many people convicted of drug offenses in prison for longer periods: in 1986, people released after serving time for a federal drug offense had spent an average of 22 months in prison.

According to UN WHO, worldwide, 30 million people a year will spend time in prison. And across all 5 continents, prison populations are growing. On any given day in 2018, more than 11 million people worldwide, including at least 410 000 children, were held in prisons –total growth of 24% since 2000. While women prisoners are still a small minority in most countries, their numbers have grown by 50% over the same period. Member States resort to imprisonment to very different degrees. While the average imprisonment rate at the global level stands below 150 prisoners per 100 000 of the national population, it reaches a rate of 300–650 prisoners per 100 000 of the national population in more than 25 Member States (1). HIV, Tuberculosis, and viral Hepatitis – notably hepatitis C virus (HCV) – are of major concern for people detained in prisons and other closed settings. Available data demonstrate that 1 in 4 detainees are HCV-positive, and the estimated global HIV prevalence in prisoners is 3% (UNODC, 2020).

Female prisoners make up 5–10% of the global prison population. They are more likely to use drugs, and their populations often have higher prevalence rates for HIV (double or more) when compared to male prisoners. Globally, the number of incarcerated women is growing, increasing by an average of 16% in the last 6 years. Women in prison are vulnerable to gender-based sexual violence. They may engage in risky behaviors and practices, such as unsafe tattooing and injecting drug use, and they are more susceptible to self-harm.

So, seeing all the above data from various sources as a society what should we do? Should we reform Police and train them to guide them to understand real crime and people who commit crimes or just let them fill the Jails/Prisons? Why is our Policing system so harsh and act like goons, pick anyone for any pity crime, prepare a case with several sections under the Law, and throw them behind bars for becoming more notorious and real criminals? What is our Judiciary doing, do they understand the case and try to apply real Law and avoid ruining the life of a person by sentencing?

The police system is creating more criminals than actual criminals on the roads or the streets. As I mentioned earlier no one is boa ca criminal, it's us the Society, the Police, and the corrupt system that makes them, criminals. Sending the person into Prison creates a very different mindset when he sees various people with n number of cases and so on around. The people in jail surrounding him make it impossible for that individual to repent or retrospect or correct what he/she has done.

Now, if say a person is in jail, what should the Police do? Below are a few things that in my perspective should be done to correct the person:

1. Understand why that person took the criminal step.
2. Empathize with the convict and give all support required medically or otherwise.
3. Have proper orientation programs in jails where a person can adapt to them and learn.
4. Introduce rehabilitation programs to correct the mindset of the convicts and give them a chance to retrospect their mistakes.
5. Rather than filling Prisons and creating facilities where people with low sentencing or low criminal record can be shown a new way of life, counselors help them to understand where they went wrong and how they can restart their new life in a better society.
6. We as a Society must accept these people and give them a chance to live and make better life rather than blame and ridicule them and put them in the Hall of Shame.
7. We need to correct our society and environment which is toxic everywhere, to avoid anyone taking a harsh or criminal step.

Finally, I want to end up by saying, let's not be judgmental about people who land up in Prisons, they were not born criminals, and we as a society turned them into such people. Accept them and reduce populating prisons where the people are not getting better but are turning bad to worse and then yes, are actual dangers to Society.

Police also need to understand the Law, and their authority and take proper precautions when arresting someone and throwing them into Prison. There are so many cases in the world where the convict is not a convict, by mistake someone else they are serving the prison sentence. Please listen to all those people, give them chance to explain and show some humanity. Police need reforms all over the Globe and their high-headedness and authority need to be curbed. They are turning into Lawful criminals and goons.

"The proud do not change to improve but defend their position by rationalizing. Repentance means change, and it takes a humble person to change." - Ezra Taft Benson

Chapter 9- Constant Craving: Digital Junkies

The smartphone is now one of our organs, not inside our body or part of our body but stuck to us in our hands and not letting it go even for a second. Our eyes are constantly glued to its screen and repeatedly scrolling various apps, games, etc. Our digital addiction has made us junkies, not of drugs but Digital screens or Digital worlds.

I had never thought that there will be a time when I will use my phone for every activity from searching to chatting to playing games or just scrolling and killing my time, it's not only me, we all are glues to this thing which is Smart Phone, I say right word chosen "Smart" because the smartness of this device made us lazy, lethargic and made us stop using our mind. We are so dependent on this device that we cannot even move from one place to another without GPS. We used to travel earlier also right, we used to go to places without GPS, we used our mind and navigation techniques and reached our destinations. But now our thinking power has gone to the toss because we cannot think and decide now, it's our smartphone that decides our thought process.

Our world has become so virtual that we have lost feelings, in a real sense. The only relationship we know now is in a virtual world, people chat with friends and family on chat apps, but when say by chance they are together they struggle to talk or express things. We have become so addicted that on our dinner table or in a restaurant, rather than enjoying a meal and time with family or friends we are stuck on Smart Screen and keep scrolling. Because our thought process is zero, we don't know what to talk about or what to talk about. People have started revolutions and debates on Twitter, WhatsApp, FB (Now Meta), and Instagram, rather than in person, isn't this bizarre? Various groups and even political system is fighting and debating on social media but not in person.

Dr. Anna Lembke, a world-leading expert on addiction in her 2021 book, Dopamine Nation, emphasizes that we are now all addicts to a degree. She calls the smartphone the "modern-day hypodermic needle": we turn to it for quick hits, seeking attention, validation, and distraction with each swipe, like, and tweet. Since the turn of the millennium, behavioral (as opposed to substance) addictions have soared. Every spare second is an opportunity to be stimulated, whether by entering the TikTok vortex, scrolling Instagram, swiping through Tinder, or bingeing on porn, online gambling, and e-shopping. "We're seeing a huge explosion in the numbers of people struggling with minor addictions," says Lembke.

Addiction is a spectrum disorder: it's not as simple as being an addict or not being an addict. It's deemed worthy of clinical care when it "significantly interferes" with someone's life and ability to function, but when it comes to minor digital attachments, the effect is pernicious. "It gets into philosophical questions: how is the time I'm spending on my phone in subtle ways affecting my ability to be a good parent, spouse, or friend?" says Lembke. "I do believe there is a cost – one that I don't think we fully recognize because it's hard to [see it] when you're in it."

We all know about Dopamine, a hormone that makes us feel happy and good and gives us a kick or thrill. Dopamine motivates us to do things we think will bring pleasure. So, using the smartphone constantly gives us that pleasure and kick, which makes us stop thinking about what it is resulting in, and the effects we are going to face from it. Although dopamine was only identified by scientists in 1957, seeking pleasure is hardwired into our brains.

With addiction, about 50% is down to genetic disposition, with the other 50% coming from environmental factors such as access, says Lembke.

Our brains haven't changed much over the centuries, but access to addictive things certainly has. Whereas our ancestors put all their efforts into seeking a mate and tasty food, we can find those, and much more besides, with the click of an app. "It's very different from how life used to be when we had to tolerate a lot more distress," says Lembke. "We're losing our capacity to delay gratification, solve problems and deal with frustration and pain in its many different forms."

We need to stop this addiction, come out of our screen, reel the virtual distracting world, start living, and divert our thought processes towards something concrete and healthy. So, the same way as the cigarette addict does, reduce the number of smokes, distract the mind to avoid those thoughts, same we must do related to digital addiction. Use less phone and start running, gym, writing, etc.

Whenever you feel the urge to open the phone, think is it important or I can do something better, I am not saying we need to stop using the phone, what I am saying is we need to stop getting glued to it, and rather utilize our time in better things. Like, in your free time rather than scrolling, listen to music, read a book, or maybe cook something for yourself. Talk to your family, and friends rather than chat. Take a step, it's important to avoid getting into junkie mode.

The purpose of that time away, says Lembke, is to reset our brain's pathways and gain perspective on how our dependency affects us. The goal is generally not to banish it forever, but to figure out how to enjoy it in moderation – that most elusive of things. Some will realize they cannot enjoy it without going too far but usually "self-binding" techniques should help with finding a balance.

Many of these ideas are familiar: we've all heard about digital detoxes and mindfulness practices, I had written an article in Digital Detox, about how we need to get ourselves out of the digital world and now I am writing again as I see the thing with people has become worse, people are walking on the road, but eyes are on screen and many met with an accident, isn't this crazy. Once, I had almost hit a girl as she was crossing the road while looking at her phone, I was furious as it would have been a mess, she would have got hurt or may be killed and I had to face the consequences. Imagine?

So, think about your mind and your health. Don't let your brain die because you are not letting it think or work. Build a real relationship with friends and family rather than getting stuck into a virtual world and feeling good factor, it's not a good factor it's a digital mess, avoid it. Start switching OFF the phones when you sleep, enjoy your weekends out, and not on the screen.

Be healthy and adopt a healthy lifestyle in the real world.

"He who has health has hope; and he who has hope has everything." – Thomas Carlyle

Chapter 10- We are Digging Our Graves – COP26

The topmost news for me was the 2021 United Nations Climate Change Conference in Glasgow. The COP26 summit has brought all parties together to accelerate action towards the goals of the Paris Agreement and the UN Framework Convention on Climate Change. All the Leaders Presidents and Prime ministers from 150 countries are present including young Climate Activists.
Everyone is talking about the damage already done to our Environment and Climate and we are on the brink of catastrophe. UN Secretary-General António Guterres, clearly mentioned Enough is Enough and we need to stop this mess, or it will stop us. We are digging our Graves. But I wonder who is digging these Graves for the whole humanity, and the answer is Big Businesses, Industrialists, and who supports their governments, so they all are responsible. These capitalists are seeing only their gains and profits, honestly, they don't care about Climate, the Environment, or People's suffering. The bitter truth and tragedy which everyone knows and people sitting in COP26 Conference.

I am curious about the outcome of what will be the final decision on the Goals laid by the UN:

1. Secure global net zero by mid-century and keep 1.5 degrees within reach

Countries are being asked to come forward with ambitious 2030 emissions reduction targets that align with reaching net zero by the middle of the century.

To deliver on these stretching targets, countries will need to:accelerate the phase-out of coal

- curtail deforestation
- speed up the switch to electric vehicles
- encourage investment in renewables.

Not sure how many countries will adopt these points, Australia is not ready as I understood from their Prime Minister, and in India, the target given to reduce carbon emission is by 2070, whereas the UN is pushing for 2050. Deforestation, checkout Brazil, Poland, and others, forests are vanishing, and who is responsible?

2. Adapt to protect communities and natural habitats

The climate is already changing, and it will continue to change even as we reduce emissions, with devastating effects.

At COP26 we need to work together to enable and encourage countries affected by climate change too:

- protect and restore ecosystems
- build defenses, warning systems, and resilient infrastructure and agriculture to avoid loss of homes, livelihoods, and even lives

Protecting the ecosystem our ocean life is dying, and it is being replaced by Plastic life. Waste material is dumped in poor countries and pollutes their places. How can one clean their house and throw waste and dirt in others' houses, is that humanity and you are accepting a cleaner environment and respect? How hypocritical, I am talking about the UK here, they are sending their wastes full of ships to countries like Romania.

3. Mobilize Finance

To deliver on our first two goals, developed countries must make good on their promise to mobilize at least $100bn in climate finance per year by 2020.

International financial institutions must play their part and we need to work toward unleashing the trillions in private and public sector finance required to secure a global net zero.

4. Work together to deliver

We can only rise to the challenges of the climate crisis by working together.

At COP26 we must:

- finalize the Paris Rulebook (the detailed rules that make the Paris Agreement operational)
- accelerate action to tackle the climate crisis through collaboration between governments, businesses, and civil society.

There are areas in various developing countries where greedy businessmen are dumping electronic waste from foreign nations. My question is why should this happen in India? Who is allowing such illegal activities, which create harm to innocent civilians? Why are criminals not punished for such illegal activities? Should not their law enforcement checks such illegal activities and stop the activity and punish the criminals as well? There is undue support from all "powerful" strata of society and that's why such criminals escape legal punishments, even if the police or para-military arrest the criminals. Law must be the first and foremost thing to be tightened in every nation. By that, citizens will fear committing heinous crimes against nature. Also, Governments need to promote encouraging programs for improving the deteriorating environment, and climate. Creating posters and spreading messages are good but are useless if people are not going to adapt and adopt them. Integrity is the mantra for the implementation of programs to change the worsening situation. Integrity is what we do when no one is watching; it's doing the right thing all the time, even when it may work to our disadvantage. Integrity is keeping our word. It's not the duty of a few but the responsibility of every human being.

2021 United Nations Climate Change Conference at Glasgow, COP26 summit is a warning to mankind to awaken and stop the ongoing nonsense. After the leaders go back to their respective homes, all nation's citizens have to follow their leader's action plans in letter and spirit.

Yes, we can rise together and work it out, but how? We need to engage every person on this earth. Make them understand what we are heading towards, we need to explain to them why we see Rains, Earthquakes, Floods, and tsunamis and what is triggering them. Mother Earth is tired and is saying Enough is Enough, I can't take it anymore, you have abused my existence and the result is what is in front of us, a disaster and catastrophe. And yes, very important we are digging our graves and for our coming generations. Let's pledge to save our environment together, save our mother earth, and heal her. We need to take steps and give something survivable and livable to our future generations so that they are thankful to us.

Today we are here and tomorrow we are gone; life is short and will not wait for you.

- Stop Using Plastic,
- Reduce the Carbon footprint by using your car once a week,
- Reduce consumption of electricity,
- Let us plant more trees and nourish them.

"The effects of climate change are real and must be acted on."- Joe Biden

Chapter 11- Is Feeling Pride a Narcissist Act?

We all have pride in ourselves and feel good about what we have achieved and somehow directly or indirectly keep talking about it. We should be comfortable owning and enjoying our achievements, big or small as it nourishes our mental health and self-esteem.

However, one of the sins I can say, pride is in many ways the most disreputable. In excess, it overshadows and engulfs the virtues of philosophy – self-reflection, critical thinking, consideration for the broader community, and the sense of one's boundedness and weakness. And yet there are also good reasons to feel more pride – it's positively correlated with life satisfaction and happiness, and negatively correlated with depression and anxiety.

There is a distinction between Self-Esteem and Pride, the latter is feeling better about yourself, whereas Pride can be thought of more narrowly, as the joy one feels due to personal or collective achievement. You can be proud of yourself or your team for winning a game or accomplishing the project and, if you identify with a team or a country that you aren't a part of per se, you can feel vivid pride through that team's or country's achievements. Self-esteem, on the other hand, represents the general assessment of oneself and what you have achieved individually which you feel proud of.

But yes, pride and self-esteem are closely related. Some of us live and die with each accomplishment and failure, causing striking fluctuations in self-esteem. Let's consider bipolar disorder, previously known as a manic-depressive disorder, in which periods of chronic low mood are interspersed with phases of intense energy. Patients with this diagnosis present with a particularly unstable sense of self. For them, a monotonous win can prompt feelings of being amazing, while an ordinary loss can provoke a devastating sense of being terrible, triggering a maniac or depressive episode, respectively, in a fraction of a second sunshine and then black thundery clouds.

Most individuals cultivate a sense of self-regard by tallying up their proverbial wins and losses. For example, I take pride in summiting the highest peak; then, if I keep summiting, I will likely come to infer that I'm a good mountaineer, thus fueling my self-esteem. In essence, one can't experience a high degree of self-esteem without first experiencing momentary pride.

When considering pride, some people conclude that it is narcissistic. Fearing hubris and an overestimation of their abilities, they simply abstain from it. To feel proud is to be self-important or worse, they fear. Especially in most religions, pride implies a sinful character. If you scroll through any of your social media feeds, you'll likely discover a tone of self-promotion, and you too might consider it narcissistic. Excessive pride can be labeled narcissistic, but the variety of pride in which one also considers her limitations is anything but pathological. The fear of pride snowballing into narcissism becomes less frightening when pride is conceived of as manageable.

The US psychologists Jessica Tracy, Richard Robins, and their colleagues further distinguish between 'authentic pride', which is grounded in specific things you've achieved through effort, and 'hubristic pride, which relates to a more general grandiose self-assessment. Similar to the individual with bipolar disorder, whose self-estimation turns with each attempt and result, Tracy and Robins, argue that hubristic pride is a form of over-generalization, wherein narrow pride leaps to a grandiose plateau. Instead of perceiving himself as a good basketball player, he might conceive of himself as the greatest of all. Often when people think of pride as unhelpful, it is this hubristic variety that they have in mind.

Pride is important to mental well-being, – specifically the authentic variety – is not only good but also necessary. What if, without it, we cease to care about ourselves? Pride is the joy of knowing that you have accomplished something you consider significant, usually because it's also significant to the broader community, but not necessarily. Pride can be found in the student who improved her grade in math class, the mother who calms her colicky child, or the football player whose team wins the Soccer match. Pride is in the ordinary and the extraordinary. Most importantly, pride helps form the foundation of mental health. People tend to imagine a life with too much pride but fail to consider a life without it.

Finally, I will close by saying, allowing yourself to feel pride boosts self-esteem, motivation, and hopefulness. All three are crucial to one's will to live, providing, in part, the 'whys' that help us carry the burdens of our suffering. When we feel proud of an achievement, we subsequently form a desire to recapture it. Additionally, pride can help us create personal ladders of success, so when you achieve anything of significance, such as trekking a small mountain, you can now consider trying a more challenging endeavor, such as summit high peaks. Finally, a sense of pride provides us with self-efficacy or the sense of our abilities. It is only by recognizing that your prior achievements matter that you can feel able to tackle future problems. The real pride, the real present, is your health and your longevity.

"If you believe in yourself and have dedication and pride - and never quit, you'll be a winner. The price of victory is high but so are the rewards."- Bear Bryant

Chapter 12- You are on Your Own

Started my day at work, as usual, not knowing what is going to happen next, what news will come, or will it be good or bad. We all go with our usual routine and manage to pass the day as it comes and hits us. Heard the news about one of my colleagues who lost his brother to neuro disease, his mother a covid patient stuck in the hospital, his father a cancer patient and on top of it, floods have ruined his home and cattle. What is he going through, and the tragedy struck him, only he knows it, no one can understand the agony and pain he is feeling.

We all face life's challenges, sometimes hard, sometimes worse and there are times when we lose hope in the existence of being in the world. These are the times when you seek support and empathy. One does not seek, but the loved ones who care for you do come at such time to be with you and be supportive. They want their friend or loved one to feel safe and not feel alone. But most of the time we see that the person who is getting through the tough times wants to be left alone, with the pain and thoughts he/she is feeling. And yes, at times they want to be surrounded by their friends and loves one whom he/she trusts and can share the pain and knows they do understand what I am going through.

Every individual in this world is going thru some sort of pain, it can be losing anything which that person is attached to or had dreamt of but didn't find or was not able to get or loss of the Loved one. Why do we always end up in pain and feeling miserable and unwanted? Why do people feel cursed and judged?

One's happiness is another person's jealousy; people are so judgmental and cruel. One cannot see the other individual content or happiness because it itches the one who feels why is this person happy and not me or why this person an has "x" thing and not me. There is always competition and race to be ahead of one another, I don't know about the West but in South Asia e.g., in India, this jealousy and competitiveness with one another are more prevalent whether between friends or relations or even among neighbors. People need to grow and be mature and have a sense of respect for one another, appreciate what others have, and feel good about it rather than saying the question, WHY?

Coming back to my topic of being on your own, as per my perspective is the reality for everyone. Say I am going through hell and it's killing me, it's only me no one can understand the real story of pain behind it which as an individual I am feeling. The other person can empathize with me and even show sympathy, but the real sorrow and pain is mine which not even my parents can see or feel. It's only an individual who undergoes the trauma. And his attached dear ones who are the real well-wishers. It's a very cruel world with a lot of people as the best actors. They will smile in front of us, and behave like really good human beings, but stab at our back. Situations in life never are easy to handle. Every new situation is a new challenge, and we need to be strong enough to be on our own. As you rightly said our dear ones can only empathize but it's the individual who must adjust the sails of his boat. Sometimes incidents so happen that even an optimistic person gets all the wildest and most negative thoughts, as one is unable to tolerate the situation. There comes the wisdom to keep calm and wait for the time to be in favor of us. Every challenge in life has to be fought by the self, and not give up hope at any time till the last. If one wants to prosper in life, he has to work harder, be smart, thinking out of the box. The others who get jealous never want to give even a try or give up in between, not availing any opportunities & that becomes the reason for the irritation of us growing up in life. Don't bother about what others think about us. Else, it will ruin our growth mindset. Keep away from such evil eyes and people. Stay with yourself, say to yourself that I need to be happy, I need to understand the situation, I need to handle it, I need to be strong enough, I need to face the toughest situation.

What a person goes through, and faces can be felt by yourself, and no one can understand that it's a reality, a fact. So, we need to be strong and know how to face tough situations. You don't need anyone to feel sorry for you or for the situation you are facing. You need yourself and understand the fact that this is my pain, and I only can and will handle this and come out of this mess as a winner. Sometimes are so hard that we can't handle it, no matter how much support we get still at the end of the day it's you and you only who need to decide what to do and how to go about it. You are enough for yourself if you know what you believe in and how to handle the circumstances and challenges you face. Be thoughtful, always think right with maturity and Be You.

"Be yourself; everyone else is already taken." — Oscar Wilde

Chapter 13- Peak Distraction

Time is going by so fast that we don't even realize what happened when and why. Each year is passing by like hours and months. We are so busy with our daily routine and things around us that what is going on and what is our priority sometimes speed away from us, why because all of us are running in a marathon where there is no end, most of the people are in this marathon even without a goal.

What are we doing, why are we getting deprived of mental peace and having no satisfaction with what we do? I have an answer for this, the only reason we are losing our mental peace is because of unnecessary DISTRACTION. And this distraction is not only taking our mental peace away but with it, we are losing our friends and running our relationships, I should say "we are failing ourselves".

So, what is this distraction, which is acting as an enemy of our life, which is taking our peace and not letting us enjoy and relax? This uninvited entity has taken so much space in our lives that we don't think of anything else except using and being with it. The main areas where we have lost interest because of this uninvited friend is:

- We eat but, we don't eat as we have full concentration on this friend
- We are with friends, physically but mentally we are not with them as our mind has been occupied by this unknown friend
- We are watching a movie or TV; however, we don't know what we are watching as we are watching stuff that our uninvited friend is sharing

- We are with our loved ones who care for us and love us, but alas, this friend who has taken a toll on our mind and life is taking us away from them and making us lose them
- Most of the hours in our daily life go with this bugger, this Mr. Distraction

Who is this, what is this distraction have you figured out by now, about whom I am talking? Yes, you are right it is no one else than our Mr. Smartphone, our Peak Distraction.

Smartphone has become the most dangerous distraction in our lives; it is spreading a disease that is worse than any other medical disease. In India itself, people are with their smartphones 04Hrs a day, this is the latest figure. We have just shunted our real life and real people and immersed ourselves in the virtual world and people. We have started being with the virtual world more than, reality around us, people being around or with us. This distraction has made us the most disrespectful creatures. We don't care what the other person sitting next to me or with me is saying as I am stuck in the smartphone and the virtual world it has created for me. We are not realizing the dangerous drawbacks this distraction is resulting IN. Majorly, health issues like eyesight going weak, headaches, backaches, losing interest in physical activities, mood swings, nausea, etc.

We now need Digital Detox, rather than Body Detox. We need to get rid of this distraction and utilize our time in physical activities, being with our friends and loved ones, and spending time with them.

Most of the relationships which are failing are because of Smartphones, this is creating a sense of distrust in your partner, your partner is not having trust in you now because he/she feels that you are with someone else on phone and vice-versa. We have lost a sense of Respect, we don't care about the other person who has come to meet us or is at the table with us as we are busy with our phones and that person loses respect for you and vice-versa if you have that sense of respect in you.

We need to stop this, what are we teaching to our future generations that are cut off from the real world and get busy with the virtual world? Don't make real friends but spend time with virtual friends. We are doing so much harm to our children, by making them use Smartphones to play games, etc., rather than letting them go to the playground or play with their friends. Now, don't give me the crappy excuse that we don't have playgrounds. We are a generation of excuses; you ask it and I have it.

Technology is good, it is for our good and future, but don't misuse it. Use Smartphones but don't get addicted to them. As we all know Access Use for Everything, or Anything is Bad. We need to use it wisely and smartly. So, let's pledge, that we will use our Smartphones in a controlled manner, we will care about our relationships and friends and families and respect them. Let's keep this Distraction aside when we are with family and friends, let's use it when required not always. Give time to yourself, you need to detox of mind and body to be fresh and to make your tomorrow better and brighter.

"One way to boost our willpower and focus is to manage our distractions instead of letting them manage us."- Daniel Goleman

Chapter 14- Fear, the Baggage

"Oh, Allah please get me back, safe and sound I don't want to die." I was bloody scared standing in that snow. Feeling weak and helpless, I was reduced to the exact opposite of who I thought I was. The mountain showed me I had a very heavy suitcase on my back that I had to offload.

On a casual working day in the office, I experienced a sudden adrenaline rush when I heard "Ready for an adventure guys? Trek to a mountain peak? Hmm? "It was Louise the professional trekker our team!

I was IN. Adventure beckoned me and I was not going to say No!

Excited about the new adventure of running up the mountains and experiencing a whole new world, we arrived at a railway station in Rabat, the platform was quiet except for some chirping of birds, no hustle bustle around, it was a beautiful sunny day, and the station was clean and good, why I am saying this is because I never boarded the train for long journeys in my country. The train arrived and we all were in first class, I was so overwhelmed about the whole trip that I forgot about what really, I was heading for.

The train was hitting the speed, I was glad until I started hearing words like" rocks, clamps, poles, summit, snow, achievement". Ah! It sounded so horrifying! So, scary! By the way, we were on our way to summit the highest peak of North Africa – Mt. Toubkal 4,167 m in all!!!

I was ready for my moment of glory, an achievement that I could tell my grandchildren. My future played out like a movie in front of my eyes, as I saw the massive Atlas Mountains spread themselves surrounding the beautiful Imlil village from where we started the climb. We started our trek from Imlil, and I being supercharged with adrenaline rushing and gushing through my veins, just wanted to fly over these mountains, and it was an amazing experience that I had never felt before. I was doing something new, something different, and something that I could talk about to others and feel proud of. After a few hours of walking in the steep Rocky Mountains, I felt breathless! My excitement and confidence vanished into thin air. The excruciating pain in my knees and back was killing me physically and mentally. I looked at the hugeness in front of me and realized that there was no turning back. Fear crept into my mind slowly.

Strangely, I was reminded of the day when I stepped on the stage to act in my first play. I had felt the same thing then, the fear. "What if I forget my lines, what will be the reaction of the audience and my director". A numbness.

My backpack of fears felt heavy on my back.

I started feeling pain in my knees and back, it was killing me physically and mentally. When I looked around, the mountains were so high like we were walking beside some huge, tall fortress wall and there was no way to turn back. As I was taking steps up towards height and low pressure, only one thing was running through my mind when will I reach our base camp and not lose my mind by any chance? Started singing songs to keep my mind occupied and reiterating to myself every second that I was not climbing the mountain which was so hard and steep but strolling on my lawn, these thoughts gave me the strength to move a bit faster.

At around 6 PM we reached our base camp "La Toubkal" which was at 10K feet. We all were wrecked, and I was not able to move or walk and even my sense of thinking was shut, totally into hibernation mode. After some rest, we moved to the dining area for tea and meals. The room was full of mountaineers "Professional" you know. There were young and old both, old as in the 60-65 age group and it was a new world to me. Looking at my condition and what I came through, I was not ready to go for the summit which we had to start at 5 AM. My negative thoughts engulfed me like dark clouds. Lou was looking at me and she read my mind and my body language about what I was going to say.

"No, Lou I can't do this I am dead, this is my summit, no more trekking and that also in deep snow, no way.

Lou looked at me and smiled as if she was expecting this! "You are my brave boy, and you have to make me proud by achieving this summit. This will be the biggest achievement of your life and you cannot run away from your promise made to me, she said. I was so scared to go for the summit as by now I had realized I was heading toward the death zone! I suffocated in the night as I was picturing myself climbing the mountains. Now, this was another baggage on my head, the baggage of fear and anxiety which I was not ready to go ahead with. These words started haunting me and my mind. Anyway, I made up my mind as I always feared something, however, tried my best to accomplish that, so will do this time too, I will make Lou and myself proud and will achieve this milestone of my life.

I don't know what made me ready to roll in the darkness of early morning the next day and finish the ultimate target of summiting Mt.Toubkal. It was Sunday 5:00 AM, base camp hiding under dark and cold morning. Lou, I, and a third member with our guide were ready to roll in the darkness of early morning and finish our ultimate target of summiting Mt. Toubkal. As we started climbing up in the dark, I felt like I am pushing myself onto the cold freezing wall and trying to put my step on it, it was a reality we were doing the same. The mountain was very steep. After trekking for 20-25 min, a ray of light appeared and we were surrounded by tall white peaks, the experience was mind-blowing, but where was the way to go up? Nowhere, was it our guide creating step marks for us to follow, yes. There was a time when I was lost, I shouted "please stop, please stop". The pain was killing me, and I wanted to crash, we found a plane surface and took a break of 4 min, Lou, tried to give me water and a few biscuits which I had denied taking and she was pushing me to take water....

"Masa, you have to drink liquid it's important, else you will be dehydrated".

We started our journey by pushing ourselves up in a queue where our guide Ibrahim was leading the way and making footsteps for us. Behind him was me, poor me and I was also doing the same because I had to create that for my other partners. My mind was not working, and I was lost, and cursing myself about why the hell I decided to the summit, am not professional, and why am I not sitting down at the base with my other 2 friends who decided not to summit. I would have been sleeping and being in my dreams in a cozy warm bed. However, with the same thought process, I was also praying, "That I want to go back safely and do not want to die in these mountains".

While crawling up, my eyes went on the marks on the snow and to my surprise, these footprint marks were of Jackals, a cold wave rushed into my spine and the reason was, a week before this adventure I had watched the movie "Frozen" in which these friends get stuck in chair car in snow and are swallowed by furious jackals. I found myself in the same situation and because of fear and losing my essential senses I was about to give up and cry loudly. Again, shouted "Stop Stop" I need rest. We all halted on the white sheet of the steep wall where nothing can be seen or heard except silence and fear. Now, at this point, I murmured "please leave me here and you guys carry on this is my summit, and I am not in a position to go further". I was crying and begging, ready to go back which was not possible at this stage or wanted to be just left there which was the same as being breakfast for jackals. I started hearing again those words, you have to do it, make me proud, you are the strong guy, and you have to achieve this for your life.

"Oh, gosh leave me alone, I am not strong, and neither am interested in achieving anything".

Like this, we stopped thrice, and I was in excruciating pain, mentally and physically. To my surprise, our guide shouted, only 5 min left to touch the summit. My eyes started searching for that peak, which we have to touch and by which I will achieve something big in my life, where I will tell the world that I made it, I was on top of the peak, top of the world, where is it? The guide shouted 3 min and we were on the edge of the peak where there was only snow that was also deep, so deep that if stuck into it, impossible to come out and you will meet death and happily hug him and no one will dare to ask you to come back to this world, ☺. I even slipped and fell into the snow on a narrow ridge. I had to pull myself out of that ditch of death.

People the summit! Our Guide said showing us the metal arch which was kept at 4,167 m.

"Hi………. Toubkal" I shouted. I did it! I made it to the summit!

Those Atlas Mountains which seemed to be like fortress the other day were under my feet today. All the mountains were looking like small, tiny peaks from the point I was standing. I was on top of the world and achieved it.

Lou looked at me and smiled. I looked at her and silently thanked her.

"Oh, Allah please get me back safe and sound. I don't want to die in these mountains had prayed. But something died that day, it was not me, it was the fear. I offloaded my baggage there and I came back alive, positive, energetic, and ready for any adventure and to push myself to further limits.

***"To overcome fear here's all you have to do: realize the fear is there and do the action you fear anyway."* — Peter McWilliams**

Chapter 15- One More Year Gone

A birthday is the anniversary of the birth of a person, or figuratively of an institution as per Wikipedia. However, I want to talk about the birthday of a person, an individual where it's a day of celebration, parties, cakes, and fun.

We all celebrate our birthdays with so much joy and fun, people wait for this day and are excited about the day, planning and deciding about it. So, a day comes, and the phone is full of birthday wishes, friends who have not been in touch with you for a full year, a message for them makes you feel good that see they still care for you and remember you. The most exciting part is at midnight, you wait to see who the first person to wish you. Excitement and happiness double when your special one or your love calls you exactly at the entry of your new day. Most people see that either their family is ready with the cake dot at 12'AM or even their friends are at the doorstep with the cake and making the Birthday special and memorable. This is the one day when you are special not only in your family, and friends but at work with your colleagues and so on. And yes, why not you should be special as it's your day and you came to this world and are enjoying every day of it.

We all know Birthdays are big business in a modern society like other special days which we have created like Mother's Day, Father's Day, Rose Day, and so on, a tactic or a gimmick from capitalist people to make people run their business and make them profitable. Everyone has one and they are celebrated religiously from the very first to the last. This wasn't always the case. Celebrating every birthday with food, gifts, and fellowship is a relatively recent development in human social society. Like so much of our modern traditions, birthdays have solid roots in old Greek and Roman traditions. The Greeks and Romans gave us the tradition of presents, candles, and parties for birthdays. There is no distinct moment in which these traditions are cemented rather it is the result of the blending of different traditions over many years.

Even if modern people don't go all out celebrating their special day, everyone knows what their birthday is and acknowledges it when it comes around every year.

However, there are "n" number of people who do not Celebrate this day as you do. Few like to keep it as usual day and don't care about it, some people feel nostalgic and want to just be with themselves and have their own space and avoid getting disturbed or they just go away from the hustle and bustle and want to feel the Solitude and immerse in it, to retrospect what they have done all these past years or that year which just passed.

Well, I am also one of them who likes to Retrospect on my life, the year which just passed away and I lost one more year of my precious life, what did I do or achieved in it. People pray and turn to the Almighty for the best wishes and blessings. I also do, turn to the Almighty and ask for forgiveness and mercy, for what may have gone wrong by me, or I may have hurt someone, or made someone unhappy. There are so many things on this day people like me do, they want to make coming years good and be blessed to do better. Few of my friends, on this special, spend time with Orphans and in Old Age Homes, because they want to give back. Spending time with Orphans gives them pleasure as they share their special day with them and make the best of it.

There are children and people in this world who don't know what a birthday means, and if they do, there is no one around them to celebrate it. We should think of them, celebrate with them, eat and exchange gifts with them and pray along with them, you never know where their prayers will take you, to the places where you never had thought of, just because of the blessings.

I am not saying that do not celebrate your birthday, what I am saying is celebrate it with some meaning. Look back at your Year gone by and do some thinking and see what you have achieved and lost. Show gratitude to the Almighty, for keeping you healthy and giving you what you asked for and expected. This is the day of self-realization and being grateful and thanking that Super-Power for giving your life and making it beautiful.

Yes, a birthday is an anniversary to celebrate and have fun but at the same time, we need to be mindful and grateful.

"Your time is limited, so don't waste it living someone else's life. Don't be trapped by dogma – which is living with the results of other people's thinking." – Steve Jobs

Chapter 16- Are we Selfish?

In one of the beautiful cities of India lived a couple Mr. and Mrs. Shah with their two kids. They were so in love with each other and made sure that they live happily and give the best schooling to their children, they had two Son.

In summers, they used to enjoy evening tea in their small garden, with various varieties of flowers blooming around, the smell of roses and dahlia and whatnot. In winters they used to enjoy warm cozy rooms full of heating. All was going well, but one day a sudden shock struck them when it was discovered that his wife had colon cancer. The world shattered around them, and everything turned dark and gloomy. Mr. Shah was clueless as to what on earth happened and why my wife. She is so caring and loving, not only caring for her family but also for others like friends, relatives, and the needy if she's around.

Mr. Shah did everything he can and tried his best to save his wife, but fate was sealed, doctors had told him that she has only a few months left, top a year. He made sure every second he is beside her and taking care of her with each breath. To take care of his wife he left his job and took pre-mature retirement because his children were still in school. One thing he made sure of is that no one tells Mrs. Shah that she has cancer. She was shocked and traumatized that what happened to her suddenly and why was she operated on. Mr. Shah told her it was just an infection a cyst that had to be removed and all will be good soon.

But towards her last phases of life, she must have understood, but kept it to her and always smiled and cracked jokes while she was in excruciating pain. She taught her husband to cook and made him prepare various recipes which she used to cook, and to her surprise, Mr. Shah turned out to be an amazing chef. Alas, a day came when she left for heaven with a smiling face as she was relieved from the pain, the pain of cancer, and this world. Mr. Shah and the children were shattered and left wondering what now, how can we imagine our home without her and who will make us laugh and love and care? But Mr. Shah told his two sons, ***"never worry about anything, nor cry. Now I am your Mum and Dad both and I will take care of you both".***

So, here is the story of what happened after he lost his beloved and better half.

Scene 1

Backdrop: Mr. Shah in his late 40's parked on a couch and was in deep thought.

Cut to: Hospital where he gets news that his wife succumbed to Cancer. He is crushed and is crying holding 2 of his kids.

Mr. Shah: Back in his thoughts,

Voiceover: I am so alone, and every day is miserable without you. I look at these walls and they are hunting me, everything is so empty without you, why did you leave us, why? How will I manage Kids and everything?

Son: Enters Room and sits next to his father.

"Dad, what will we do now, how will we manage", I am missing mummy."

Mr. Shah: You don't need to worry about anything, remember now onwards, I am your dad and I am also your Mummy. We will manage everything, remember if we become weak and loose, people will take advantage of that, do you understand what I am saying?

Son: Yes, Dad. Don't worry I will be strong.

Mr. Shah: Good, that's my boy.

Scene 2

Backdrop: Mr. Shah is sitting in his office and working.

Colleague: Hey, how are you doing? Sorry to hear about your loss.

Mr. Shah: That's all right, you cannot change fate. It was supposed to happen, and I was prepared for it.

Colleague: You are strong indeed, btw, how are the kids doing? They will be missing their mother. It is tough for them.

Mr. Shah: Yea, very tough. But I am there for them and will take care, as I was when she was sick.

Colleague: Can I suggest something if you agree?

Mr. Shah: What?

Colleague: You are young and your whole life is in front of you, kids are also growing and they need both parents.

Mr. Shah: What are you trying to suggest to me?

Colleague: Why don't you give a thought about remarriage, I am not saying immediately but just give it a thought and see if you, maybe you will find someone who will take care of you and your kids.

Mr. Shah: Not sure, and it's too early.

Colleague: I understand, just had a thought rest all is up to you. Take care.

Scene 3

Backdrop: Mr. Shah's home and he is thinking about what a colleague discussed with him at work.

Mr. Shah: At the dinner table and having dinner with his kids. "I need to talk about something with you both, it's just a thought, OK?"

Kids: Ok

Mr. Shah: You see, I was doing a lot of thinking and had a suggestion from my friends about ... mmmm about getting married again. Because you guys need a mother and someone who can take care of the home.

Son: No, we don't need any stranger to come and take place of our mother.

Kid2: I agree, we can manage ourselves. We don't need a new Mummy.

Son: No one can replace our Mummy.

Mr. Shah: I understand but say tomorrow when you guys will be busy with your life and work and family, I may need someone to talk to share my daily stuff. Don't you think so?

Son: Do you understand what these new Mothers do, they break the family, one of my friends has gone thru this and he is now living with his grandparents. He lost his dad and his home.

Mr. Shah: All cannot be the same. There are exceptions.

Son: In this area, they all the are same, either they will come with their children or will have and will care about their ones and we will become strangers and stepchildren, I don't accept that and will never let that happen in our lives.

Kid2: Dad, why are you worried? You have us and we will take care of you, don't you trust us and we will live happily.

Mr. Shah: I trust you and love you both. Ok, as you both say I won't think about remarrying again. I have you and we have us.

Scene 4

After a few years. Mr. Shah has grown old and is just struggling with things, is retired now and sitting at home. Kids have grown and are busy with their lives, wives' work, etc.

Mr. Shah: He feels alone and is sometimes scared to ask for help or anything from his Son etc. He does not have anyone to talk to.

Mr. Shah: To son, listen I have to see a doctor today, will you come early from the office and take me to a clinic?

Son: Dad, I will try but as you know I am very busy.

Mr. Shah: that's all right, I will manage myself. (Mr. Shah, thinks wish I had remarried, at least my wife would have been here to take care of me and at least give me company).

Scene 5

After a few months, Son realizes his father is struggling with various things, and he needs someone to be with him, as a partner, someone to share his thoughts and spent time with.

Son to the camera: I was so selfish, now I am realizing that we should have let Dad remarry, he would have someone to be at his side and take care of him. We all become selfish at every step of life and try to play safe so that we don't get affected. Do we at that time think about our loved ones and what they will be going through? We always think about ourselves and want our happiness, jeopardizing the life and happiness of others and in my case, my father.

We should always keep in mind that they also deserve to live and be happy, if your parents can sacrifice their life for your happiness, why can't you?

In the end, I want to say only one thing "Live and Let Live"

Chapter 17- Bad Management

I am tired of my manager, always micromanagement. I am done with my Boss and am going to talk to HR about the way employees are treated. My manager is useless, he does not know anything and tries to expect us to do everything on time, does he know what this work is all about, what process we follow? I am done, and putting down my papers, can't work with such a Manager and management like this.

So, have anyone of you also had such feelings and thoughts about your manager or your Boss? I am sure yes, there are instances when you feel your boss is not doing justice to you and is expecting too much from you. We also feel that we are doing everything as expected for my job, but I am not given full credit for that, or my being a good employee has been never appreciated by my manager. This is true and honestly, even I have felt the same in my earlier days when I was new to the industry and corporate world. But have we ever thought are we right in making such remarks or making a judgment about our immediate boss? What if you were in their position and how you would have handled the situation which you are in, would you have done something different, well I doubt it, and depends on the situation.

We all sulk, crib, and judge the other person who is managing us or you are reporting to, I can say 85% of employees are not happy with their management and there are various factors responsible for that which I will discuss in another article. But we have never tried to be in our manager's shoes and see things from his/her perspective, why because they are also answerable to someone, and they do have their limitations.

So, here are a few areas where we need to work on and focus to have a good relationship with your manager:

Communication: Very fundamental principle in any relationship, is communication. Do we talk and discuss where we need to work? If your manager is not happy with your work or performance, did you ever speak about it, did you try to set up a One-on-One meeting with your manager and discuss why he/she has this perception or what triggered this, your manager is observing you, there may be instances where you may need to focus ON. So, start communicating about your performance once a month, get feedback on how you are doing, etc., and vice versa.

Visibility: You are doing a wonderful job, and your peers are so happy with your work as you help them and share your expertise, the best thing, your client appreciates your contribution, and you observe your manager is not bothered about all this and when it comes to performance review you don't get what was expected by you. Why reason is you and only you because you never highlighted your good work. When you are doing good work make it visible, show your manager your initiatives and what you do for the team, or when you get client appreciation share with your manager, if its verbal appreciation, request for same on mail and forward that to your 1st Line and 2nd line Manager. This is called being in limelight, if I am doing good work why won't I talk about that, you should.

Feedback: Always ask for feedback from your peers, your stakeholders for your work who are involved in day-to-day business, Clients, Management, etc. who deal with you and know that you are contributing the best of knowledge and you are fit for your work. Make sure this feedback is in black & white and then share the same with your manager.

Work/Data: We work so hard every day and make sure that we meet our deadlines and deliver on time. We make sure not or never to miss SLAs and be the best of the breed. But do we keep track of our work, do we have our data points ready when appraisal time will come, and I can prove my work? I remember a few years back when I was working for Dell, we had a points system for all employees and at the end of the month top 50 employees were announced and among them, the top 10 were the best breed of that month. This one time I knew coming month I will be the No.1 and was waiting for the list to come out and flash on the board, I had my data points measured and had met all the points in metrics to have the top spot, however when the list was uploaded to my shock, I was No.10, you can say wow still you made top 10. No, wrong as I already said I had all my data points ready, and I should be at Top of the list. You know I straight met with my Senior Delivery Manager and discussed my rating for the month, he was so happy to see me and my passion, he made reporting team relook at the whole list of 800 people and see where errors have happened. And you know when the new list was out, I was No.1 for that month.

So, how all this happened, I made sure I do the best of best. Worked in such a way so that no one questions my capability be it, anyone. Always made the point that my work speaks for me and most importantly my data points are ready with me.

Finally, we came to an end and what we learned is, always note what you do and keep a record of that. Most important always ask for feedback. When you set clear communication and expectations, and make your work visible, like this, we will never complain, or say my manager is bad or he/she does not understand me, or is having undue expectations, or never appreciates my efforts. Remember, always your manager is not wrong, you can be at fault too. You may be the best at your work but say you missed the SLA or you missed the timeline for the presentation. Tomorrow you will be also Manager and managing employees, so imbibe the above points and share the same with your direct reports.

"Respect for ourselves guides our morals, respect for others guides our manners. ..."

Chapter 18- Reality and Dream

There are two issues here: one is the degree to which an experience seems subjectively real (at least while it is happening). The other issue is independent of the first; this is the degree to which the experience seems objectively real in the sense that it produces actual effects on other parts of reality.

Since the age of 14, I was more mature than my other friends. I realized what is good and bad, what we should do, and why. I had embraced my Solitude and was happy being in it.

There was only one person behind my mature brain, and she was my mother. She always wanted me to learn things whether cooking, cleaning, or understanding life. I used to run away from things that she used to tell me to do and her advice always used to be,

"You have to learn, what if tomorrow you move to a new place, how you will manage".

My brother never had to go through this process of learning. I used to be angry with him as he was free to go out play and do whatever he wants. With time and me growing up, things changed I was more of a homely guy rather than being out and being with friends. Started being alone with myself in my room, studying, think all the weird things on earth. And the best stuff I used to think about was being Superman or some special guy with loads of extra powers. Why those thoughts and feelings because I wanted to run away from the whole scenario.

One fine day, my mind was boiling with all the weirdest thoughts, I was on a roller coaster of misery and helplessness, not sure why my thoughts and my inner self were in some sort of trauma and denial of my existence. And in this whole pull and push, I found myself drenched in snow and running from everything in a void where there was no destiny or goal. Ran away from my home and decided not to come back. But, after a day-long walking and moving from one place to another crying and cursing and saying sorry to my parents, there was a time when suddenly I found myself lying in my bed. How did I come back, what was that force which made me return to home, I don't know, but it was a real miracle.....

My mum was always worried about me and wanted me to be happy as she loved me more than anything else. We were like best friends, laughing, and talk, and sharing everything. She was my mentor and guide and taught me everything that I am today. She treated me like I was her daughter rather than a son. Maybe she wanted to have a daughter and I was born. It was more of a mother-daughter relationship rather than a mother-son relationship. Sometimes I wonder if was I her daughter and by mistake took shape of a boy when I was born.

As a lonely lad, always in my thoughts and solitude, playing with all things which do not exist and being with my imaginary friend had a different effect on me. I loved to be with myself and in my fantasy world. Being not so connected to people around and having no friends, I decided to move to a different city or place. And my parents agreed for me to be sent to Delhi for the rest of my schooling and college. This was a turning point in my life, no one was around me I was in my world. Learned to be independent and tackle things on my own, from a shy guy who became smart, with a tremendous presence of mind.

I started writing letters to my mum, as at that time there were no mobile phones. She used to write me back everything which we used to talk about in person, we started talking through letters. I started growing up and being more confident, mature, and responsible. Being away from my folks and with no one to bother me, I was bound to do anything, and I could have even turned to bad company or friends because it was my way out. But never did that always maintain a distance from groups who were troublemakers or can deviate me from my studies. This again used to come from my mum's letters, my parents had trust in me and knew their son will not disappoint them or will not do anything which will break their trust. And parents should have this feeling and faith toward their kids. If you cannot build that trust or faith, your child will think in a reverse manner.

Being a happy and confident guy, I was good at my studies and besides my regular school and college, was doing my extra activities related to Radio, Television, and most important Theater. Everything I was doing was teaching me some or the other lesson and yes thanks to my mum and dad being my support at every step and decision I took. I understood the meaning of life and what it means. I grew up with a different personality, self-confidence, and independence.

My Solitude helped me a lot in this whole personality development and growing into a mature man.
Alas, there was a day when my Mum was diagnosed with Colon Cancer, I was shattered, my world came crashing

down, and it was a sudden earthquake on a scale of magnitude that no one can imagine or calculate. Doctors gave a time frame of a year for her survival, it was all done and dusted and there was no hope. I was watching my Mum, dying in front of me day in and day out but nothing I can do except loads of prayers and beg Allah to give her back to me. As I had stepped into the world of work and earning, so had to be in Delhi. Always used to talk to her on the phone laugh and giggle and make jokes as we used to do. And one day on phone she said, "People come, people leave and that's how the world ends", after a few days of that saying, my phone rang and I knew what the news was about, and that was the end.

My Mother and my best friend left me in the void, now with whom will I share my ups and downs, my laughs, and my achievements? And a miracle happened, one day I woke up with confusion and happiness. Guess what, I just had finished talking to my Mum, not through letters or phone but face to face as we used to at home and whatever regular was happening, we discussed that.

What was it, a reality, or a dream? I wondered if it was a dream however, the talks and discussion were real. She has never stopped talking to me since then and I always share things with her as I used to do always.

So, as I mentioned there are two issues here: one is the degree to which an experience seems subjectively real (at least while it is happening). The other issue is independent of the first; this is the degree to which the experience seems objectively real in the sense that it produces actual effects on other parts of reality. Both the issues happened to me, and I am happily living and experiencing them.

Chapter 19- World of AI (Artificial Intelligence)

Well, everyone is talking about AI these days, few support it, few admire this new technology and some of them are feeling not good about it and are a bit skeptical. Now, skeptical in what way, there are various areas where I also somehow feel a bit scared of this technology, so the areas are:

a. More machine intervention in any Sector or Industry, resulting in job losses
b. More threat to systems because of cyber threats, which is increasing a lot
c. Maybe machines or robots will not be able to understand the situation in critical conditions, because they were not coded that way, in areas of self-driving or medical field
d. Major threat in case of ammunition or military side if AI involved that side

According to experts, there are three major areas where we see the threat in terms of Artificial Intelligence, Drones turned into missiles, Fake Videos manipulating public opinion, and Automated Hacking which I mentioned in the above points, and this happens if the technology goes into wrong hands and which we must be aware of. Policymakers need to put thinking caps related to these issues as to how this can be avoided. While AI researchers and architects are working on this, they also should be aware and proactive about if it goes into the wrong hands and how to handle it.

Now, let's talk about the jobs and people scared of this new technology and feeling insecure about their future. A report from Forrester predicted that by 2021, intelligent agents and related robots will have eliminated a net 6% of jobs. That's a huge number. We must understand that when tasks are automated, becoming cheaper and faster, we need more human workers to do the other tasks in the process that haven't been automated. So, for that we need to work on acquiring more skills or upskilling ourselves, our employees need to be ready for future jobs. If an organization is planning to acquire AI and newer technology, then you need to first work and think about how to upskill your existing employees and what skills they need, we cannot just start laying off people or saying your service is no longer required now.

So, the most important point is you all need to think about new skills and expertise where you can grow. In the present world you cannot survive on your old or existing skills, keep upgrading yourself as we upgrade the system, etc. this is the need of an hour.

As per, @Max Tegmark, President of the Future of Life Institute, the top myths of AI or Advanced AI can be seen below diagram, he has very accurately mentioned the Myths and Facts about it, which is very helpful and relief, I can say,

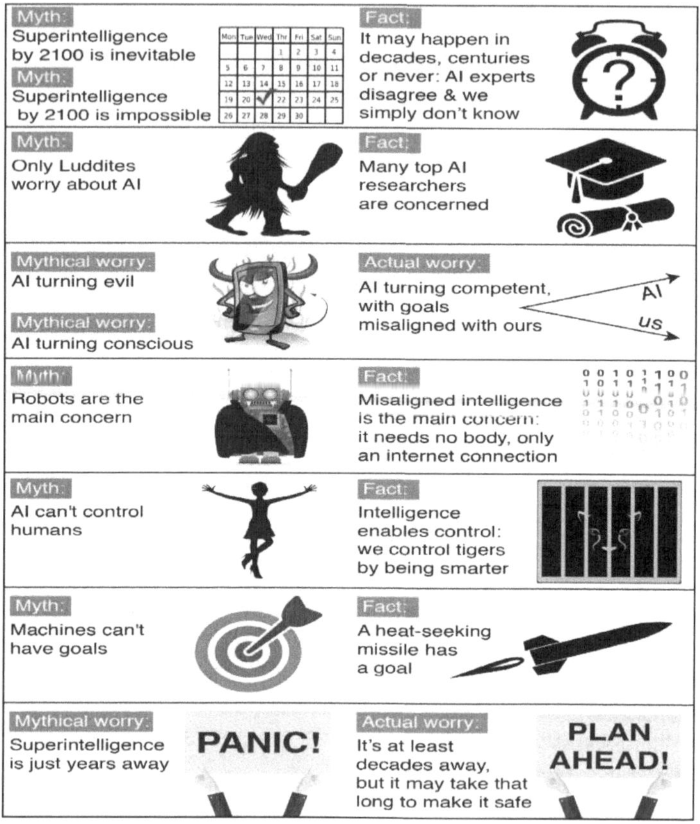

Lastly, will AI or Robots take over human intelligence, and what will be the consequences? Well, as per research and experts this is not going to happen soon or in near future, however, this may happen down the line say 100 years or 200 years, so it is centuries away. As of now, whatever we are feeding into AI systems or AI Robots, or Super AI robots is working accordingly and needs a lot of human intervention. So, we need to make sure whatever algorithms and codes are written are accurate and have security features. There are a lot of myths related to AI which are just rumors, however, as people see them as risks and concerns, in that case, AI researchers should take them seriously and work on them and make them safe.

The AI or robot misconception is related to the myth that machines can't control humans. Intelligence enables control: humans control tigers not because we are stronger, but because we are smarter. This means that if we cede our position as the smartest on our planet, we might also cede control. We, humans, made AI technology, we are behind the Robotics, so we know how to control them and it's our brain and intelligence behind these innovations.

We will control this new technology and guide it and not the machines or robots. We are Smart and Intelligent, not machines. However, now with some machine learning techniques such as deep learning in neural networks, it can be difficult or impossible to understand why the machine is making the choices that it makes. In other cases, it might be that the machine can explain something, but the explanation is too complex for humans to understand, and it happened with a few companies where they were not able to explain to the people what is going on rather than tried to brush it under carpet. One more concern is about the AI being biased, for example, in areas of criminal punishment to photograph captioning. These biases are more than just embarrassing to the corporations which produce these defective products; they have concrete harmful effects on the people who are the victims of these biases, as well as reducing trust in corporations, government, and other institutions which might be using these biased products. As of now algorithmic bias is one of the main threats in AI and will remain so in the future unless we endeavor to make our technological products better than we are, it's us, humans, what we feed to the system that get the desired output. There are various issues related to AI technology that somehow is scaring everyone.

Every time innovations or technologies are introduced to the world, it always creates something good which helps people and the world, makes things better and easier, and yes, AI offers those same amazing new abilities but to make the world a better place we need to choose to do that, in accord with ethics. We need to understand what is right and what is not, and does this gets implemented ethically, so there is no bias of any kind.

"I do not believe in the immortality of the individual, and I consider ethics to be an exclusively human concern with no superhuman authority behind it." - Albert Einstein

Chapter 20- Ramadhan- The Month of Fasting

Ramadan, Arabic Ramaḍān, in Islam, is the ninth month of the Muslim calendar and the holy month of fasting. It begins and ends with the appearance of the crescent moon. For Muslims, Ramadan is a period of introspection, communal prayer (ṣalāt /namaz) in the mosque, and reading of the Qurʾān. God forgives the past sins of those who observe the holy month with fasting, prayer, and faithful intention. By the Grace of the Almighty. I also strictly kept my fasts and made sure I observe them with good faith and that what is mentioned to us followed during this one month.

Ramadan, however, is less a period of atonement than it is a time for Muslims to practice self-restraint, in keeping with ṣawm (Arabic: "to refrain"), one of the pillars of Islam (the five basic tenets of the Muslim religion). Although ṣawm is most commonly understood as the obligation to fast during Ramadan, it is more broadly interpreted as the obligation to refrain between dawn and dusk from food, drink, sexual activity, and all forms of immoral behavior, including impure or unkind thoughts. Thus, false words or bad deeds or intentions are as destructive of a fast as eating or drinking. So, one purifies its soul, mind, and heart to avoid above mentioned things. I feel like a new person and my spiritual side dominates more than thinking about worldly things.

For example, there are additional prayers offered at night called the tawarīḥ prayers, preferably performed in the congregation at the mosque. During these prayers, the entire Qurʾān may be recited over the month of Ramadan. To accommodate such acts of worship in the evening, work hours are adjusted during the day and sometimes reduced in some Muslim-majority countries., so I dropped going to the Gym rather than observing my tawarīḥ salat. It just appeared to me that it's best this month to observe my salat which will make me closer to Allah and I can pray more, maybe my prayers will be answered and that is my belief and faith.

Ṣawm or to refrain can be invalidated by eating or drinking at the wrong time, but the lost day can be made up with an extra day of fasting. For anyone who becomes ill during the month or for whom travel is required, extra fasting days may be substituted after Ramadan ends. Volunteering, performing righteous works, or feeding the poor can be substituted for fasting if necessary. Able-bodied adults and older children fast during the daylight hours from dawn to dusk. Pregnant or nursing women, children, the old, the weak, travelers on long journeys, and the mentally ill are all exempt from the requirement of fasting.

Fasting is a deeply spiritual experience sanctioned by the Islamic faith, but medical experts also point out neurological and nutritional benefits for the human body and brain. Essentially, fasting cleanses our body of toxins and forces cells into processes that are not usually stimulated when a steady stream of fuel from food is always present. When we fast, the body does not have its usual access to glucose, forcing the cells to resort to other means and materials to produce energy.

"If an individual cares about having regular sleep, regular nutrition, and other regular movements of life, he/she will capitalize on the benefits of fasting in Ramadan more than others," said Murat Alemdar, an associate professor of neurology at the Medical School of the Sakarya University.

Fasting also helps the brain rest during a period when other organs of the human body such as the stomach are less in use because eating, drinking, smoking, and other related activities come to a halt in Ramadan, according to Alemdar.

"In a period, when less nutrition enters the human body, leading to other organs to send much fewer signals to the brain [where more than 100 billion nerves communicate with each other constantly to ensure the body to function in a proper sense] and help it rest a little more than other times," Alemdar said.

In a spiritual sense, the brain also rejoices when the nervous system believes that something important for life has been fulfilled by fasting, Alemdar says.

Fasting can also help the body fight conditions like oxidative stress, which can increase the possibility of cancer, slowing the speed of the spread of cancer cells," Kucukvardar observes. But for many nutritionists, the most important gain of fasting could be weight loss, I lose 04 to 05Kg every Ramadhan and it's a fact. I feel so light and good.

Finally, being a Muslim I observe the fasts during the month of Ramadhan, from my perspective, the whole truth behind this is it gives me a feeling of peace due to a fulfilled mission in a field of worshipping which brings tranquility, creating positive effects on my brain and same happens to all people who observe fasting, Fasting liberates the brain from many other daily activities, increasing the prospects of its concentration on essential functions in the nervous system," Alemdar observed, citing reduced anxiety in Ramadhan.

Your sincere prayers, your devotion, and your faith in Allah will make you a better human to serve this society with wisdom and truth. I am praying that happiness will find you as you are walking down the street. Ramadan Mubarak!

References: TRT Magazine; Britannica.com.

Chapter 21- Education System in India

Education is the most important element for all societies, it is very crucial that every country provides the best education to their young students and on top of that is affordable so that all can get it rather than just a few who can afford it.

Indian young brains move out to other countries for higher education, like masters, doctorates, etc. and mainly they go to the UK, Europe, America, Canada, Australia, etc. However, Russia/Ukraine war has opened the pandora box concerning Indian Education System. Why are so many Indian students studying in Ukraine? Or elsewhere? Are they not getting a quality education here in their own country, or is there any other reason? Honestly, I was shocked to see the pictures and videos of these students in thousands trying to come out of various cities of Ukraine and thinking so many of our young brains are outside.

The question comes now, why do we see so many young bright brains running out of India for their education? I got an answer from one of my friends when I asked this question, and he was right saying, firstly, it's so expensive to study in a good college in India and in certain specific streams the cut-off for getting admission is so high that normal average student cannot get into it, even if he/she wants to. Secondly, the education system in India is flawed and most of the curriculum is outdated, right this is surprising, and I don't know what our department of education is doing about it, or are they even aware of this and thinking of fixing it? There are "n" several private colleges and universities in India that provide various degrees in medicine, management, engineering, and whatnot. But are they doing justice to these students, because it's clear the students who are not able to get into these premium colleges where the cut-off is so high, opt for these private colleges, and then also it becomes evident how much they will be paying the fee to get into these institutions, why I smell corruption at the high scale? What is the Government doing to keep a check on these private intuitions or are they one of the areas for rich politicians and businesspeople to make their black money white? Think?

Also, do these institutions provide quality education to the students so that they see their future bright? Because these students want to see their future in big Corporates, Hospitals, etc. they want to see their future growth with the right education in the stream they are studying and specializing in. Students and all young people want to see the best they can do with good and respectful living. Recently, we saw how young students were protesting in Bihar and UP related to their exams for Government Jobs. As per them, they prepare for these competitive exams for years, living away from their families, and at the end when exam time comes the papers are "Leaked", and they can't appear for the so-called exam and are left in uncertainty and confusion. And we have seen devastating results of this, anxiety, depression, suicide, and dejection from life. There are no jobs at all, youth is struggling to survive, and they are clueless about what to do with their future and where to go.

So, parents who can afford to send their children outside India to study and make the future they do, and the poor cannot do it, so they are left struggling on the streets and keep applying for Government jobs which are Zero. Only rich and upper-middle-class Indians who can afford premium institutions and Universities in India get the best education and the rest who can afford to go out of India as they have hope, rest fall through the cracks. Now, back to my question about where our Education System is heading, is our government aware of this disaster, do they know there is a major system flaw that needs to be fixed? There is so much bias in society concerning who gets better education and who will not, are they aware, they are aware, but no one is doing anything. Let the system run as it is, why bother and who is suffering, yes, our youngsters, out the truth, our bright shining Minds who are actual future of our country which will make us powerful in the world. If our youth is not educated well and is doing constructive job and work, then not only their future is dark but at the same time, our Country is headed to a dark future.

Finally, my perspective on our education system is that our society needs to do deep and serious thinking, Parents and Educationists need to come together and work on making our colleges and universities affordable to all. There should be no Cut-Offs in 99% and more, be reasonable. All cannot go out of the country for studies, and those who are leaving are going because of not getting good college in India. The government of India must make new policies and have a better strategy to make sure all students get the latest and best education here so that we stop Brain Drain from India.

"The function of education is to teach one to think intensively and to think critically. Intelligence plus character - that is the goal of true education." - Martin Luther King, Jr.

Chapter 22- No One is Busy

Anytime you want to contact an individual either you get a response I am busy as of now or can you please contact me later as I am occupied right now? Even I do the same sometimes if I am occupied with work or some activity. But not always right, are we so busy always, every time that we can't give time to our near and dear ones.

People say they are choked with work and don't have time, always busy like crazy. Is this true? I don't think so, because if one knows how to manage their time and how to prioritize the work then no one can be busy. Or what one can say is the person does not want to talk to me and is avoiding me for the same reason. And it is true if you want to avoid someone troubling or nagging then either you don't pick up the phone or meet or just totally ignore them.

We have to make balance and understand what needs to be done and when. Giving an excuse by using "BUSY" does not solve the purpose. Most people are fiercely defensive about their busyness. We have processes to streamline, goals to accomplish, promotions to earn, debt to eliminate, exercise regimes to master, dreams to chase—and hopefully along the way, people to help and inspire. Everyone is in a race where we are all occupied not with our happiness and well-being but to impress others and get inspired. If one is a famous personality and is trying to share the mantra of success that does not mean one needs to look at their mantra and start doing it, it will not happen. You need to work on your persona and think about your plus and minus points and work on them efficiently and effectively.

We multitask, even when it means not truly being present in an activity we enjoy, and maybe even feel guilty for blocks of unplanned time in our schedules. We look for productivity hacks and apps, join forums to discuss ways to get more things done; and when we do aim to simplify our lives, even that undertaking involves a lengthy to-do list. Working reality doesn't have to be so painful that we can't wait to escape it. If we follow our bliss, we can fill our days with work that stretches us, fulfills us, and endows life with a whole new level of meaning. Squeezing more into your day often detracts and derails one from its ability to be effective in each situation. One needs to prioritize the schedule in such a way that rather than doing 30 things at one time and reaching nowhere to doing at least the best 05 activities which will make you close to your goal and then realize yes, you have achieved the milestone.

One should always know their priorities, everything one does may not have urgent priority as we think so. It's a human tendency to get stressed to see a lot on the plate and sometimes end up doing nothing which turns into chaos. So, always remember to:

- Have a list of things to do on daily basis written on a notepad etc.
- Arrange the items in order of urgency or priority.
- Never jump from one item to another, always finish one and go to another.
- If you are good at multitasking, then do smaller items with the least priority.
- Review the work which you have completed and move to another.

- Always read all your emails in your mailbox and keep them clean and tidy.

Have sticky posts on your board and set them as a visual board to have the idea of how much work is done and how much is left, be Agile, and organized. Think about what it is you're seeking and what might be the most direct path to get it. Then realize that sometimes doing less can pave the path to experiencing more—more satisfaction, more ease, and even more effectiveness and efficiency. Always have a smile on your face and be positive whether at work or doing other stuff apart from work, if you work under stress, it will get stuck. When we wrap our days around things, we must leave very little time for the things we want to do. Happiness requires a balance.

We need time with the people we love. We need space to do the things we enjoy without any agenda other than having fun. We need opportunities to disconnect our minds and experience the world with childlike curiosity and wonder. All of this requires us to whittle away at our busy schedules and busy timetables which are worthless.

These are a few tips from my day-to-day life and the way I like to work. Hope you will start the same way and see the change in your style of working. See I am not advocating that we shouldn't have and pursue goals. And also, not suggesting that we should find ways to avoid work. We can transform ourselves and our lives not just through the results of our hard work but through the efforts themselves. We all can create a reality that is not just a means but an end in itself. It starts by asking ourselves a few very important questions to be sure our efforts support our true intentions:

- What is it I want to accomplish and achieve?
- What can I do today that supports my deepest passions and goals?

Think about yourself and your life, I have written about what if we are going to die tomorrow, so keep that in mind and imagine you have limited time in this world, what will you do, and what will you prioritize? So, I am sure now you will not say I am busy and invest your precious time more efficiently and effectively. Give time to yourself, and your loved ones and shine in the world.

"It's called an occupation. Not a preoccupation. It's called a success, not an obsession. And it's called being in a business. Not being in abyss-ness. It's called giving yourself a break to avoid a breakdown. It's called being good to you."- Karen Salmansohn

Chapter 23- Game of "Throne", Or "Survival"

New Technology and New Flaws, every day we see "n" number of products being launched, and companies are competing with each other to remain stable in the market. It's like a game or a race, a Game of Survival, Survival of the Best. There is no time for a Product Company to sit back and relax and watch its product for a few years to see how it is doing. They cannot have that liberty now if you are relaxing, the next moment your competitor will take over, and your product will be out of the market, and so will your company.

The question is how this race proceeding is, are these products really good to compete in the market be it mobile phones, cars, or any other product? When Samsung launched Galaxy Note7, it was a WOW thing but because of the battery issue they had to recall the product from the market, and as a user, I will say they failed their customers, and their market image got a setback. According to the electronic giant, around 500,000 replacements happened which is huge. The recent survey was done, and the results foreshadow tougher times for Samsung after the 1 million phone recall, which analysts predict could cost the world's biggest smartphone seller $904 million.

Now, in this race #, Apple is never behind #Samsung, they are launching new series of phones and the most recent one is the "x" series. So, what do we expect from this product, how are consumers looking at it, are they flawless and with no issues, maybe or maybe not, my fingers are crossed. Introducing new products in the market because the competitor is rushing new products makes you jeopardize the quality. Companies do blame third-party service providers for their failure of the product, but do they realize that it was because of their pressure and rush to achieve the deadlines which worsened the quality? Who suffers at the end of the day, it's the customer who has to consume that product.

As per the markets and the way consumer understands the product, the product is made. In developed countries, the company cannot afford to introduce cheap stuff, but the same company uses the cheaper quality in developing countries.

According to me keeping in mind this mad race of survival, companies are losing on Quality and Testing. Are all checking and monitoring the products before throwing them into consumers' hands and making sure work? Who is responsible for this mess? For a couple of years, we have seen products being recalled because of tiny issues which end up in havoc, like from automobile industry Toyota, Volkswagen, Honda, and yes Tesla and Mercedes are not behind, recalling their cars because of various issues.

Why is this madness, why can't they do a proper Test and Quality check on the Product before launching it in the market? What this all is resulting in, Customer Dissatisfaction and losing loyal consumers and clients, Brand Image Crash, and making the Competitor WIN the Game, the Game of Survival.

"Play to win, not "not to lose"."

There are other observations also, which are the contributor to the failed quality of the products and organizations need to focus on such areas. There is new technology in the market, new ways of working, and so on. Keeping this in view, do companies focus on training and upskilling the staff and introducing new technologies? After Covid-19 we have seen that there is so much stress and pressure on the workers. Because of the undue influence of health issues and an unhealthy work environment, people are leaving their jobs, as I have mentioned in my earlier chapter about "Great Resignations". This is affecting the companies, be it manufacturing, retail, transportation so on and so forth. Companies are seeing a shortage of people because of this trend where people are moving out of pressure cooker environments. Now, to fill those positions, organizations need to find skilled labor, where in the market there is a lack of skilled/trained workforce, which again is affecting production. Due to this work pressure, and undue deadlines, people take shortcuts and jeopardize the product quality, and we see a lot of issues in the end product due to human error.

Apart from human error and unqualified personnel, then we have one more major issue that is related to the machinery/machines. The company introduces new machines but failed to understand that they don't have the capability in-house to run these new sophisticated machines. These machines need to be maintained and looked after; it costs money. Because of uncertainty in the world order nowadays, with War, etc, the availability of spare parts is not readily available, and companies have to wait for replacement parts. Recent chaos is related to the chip market, chips are not available, then comes the lithium for the batteries, everything is so unavailable that car manufacturers are not able to get their new products out in the market on time and there are frequent delays, apart from that most importantly the prices are going higher and higher due to shortage. Some companies are still using old and outdated technology, and because of this there is wear and tear which is frequent and spare parts or upgrades are not available. And this issue is related to the IT software also, companies still are using WIN-98, etc. so they are so in a legacy environment that is tough to maintain, and it affects the production and quality of the product.

With the old technology and old machinery in place, the question arises about workplace safety. Companies ignore the safety area and just want the products to be made and sent out to the market. There are so many accidents that happen in such environments and are swept under the carpet. When the machines are running 24/7 and have an excessive workload, there has to be wear and tear and failures which again affect the delivery and the quality.

As I mentioned earlier about the cheap materials used in the products, companies do take the hit, and sometimes because of low-grade materials, there are fatal accidents, for which these companies pay heavy penalties. There are a lot of variations, defective materials, and most of the time inadequate testing and lack of standardization. There is a lack of coordination among suppliers because companies rush with undue expectations from the suppliers this issue comes up, lack of communication with suppliers, no handshake or understanding. There are countries where we see tremendous corruption and that results in unreliable source which supplies the wrong specification and lack attention to detail. When the focus is not given to testing and quality, companies see design errors, faults in product flows, etc.

Companies where the management is good and understand the product and the customer perform well in the market. Not only does the company performs but the people working in such organizations are loyal and always innovate and come up with new ideas.

However, if the organizational management does not have a vision, they lack the mission and value system, and they suffer. Failing to identify/understand customer needs/requirements is a major setback for the organization, if that is not taken care of on time, there is a definite downfall of the organization. Always, we need to understand the brand fails because of the management failure and their lack of commitment and values. People if they compete within and Management start showing favoritism which is wrong, they feel this is the way to survive and be visible in the company, where I say your work and ownership and dedication should make you visible and the best in the organization. There are instances where the bad decisions of the management board lead to the failure of the product, say for example the product was launched without understanding the design, lack of strategy in building the product, or people don't understand the intent behind the decision made and lack the communication skills.

Some more areas where the management fails to understand the product and decision-making are:

- No knowledge of process understanding
- Lacking fact-based decision making
- As mentioned earlier bad design decisions
- Unrealistic schedule to meet the deadlines
- Not providing adequate tools or manpower
- Miscommunication between departments and various teams
- Too much emphasis is placed on short-term results at the expense of long-term goals
- No accountability or ownership whatsoever
- No one responsible for the overall success of the project
- Conflict of interest

We know companies or organizations compete and make sure what solutions they provide are world-class and no other competitor is capable of copying or coming up with such product, let it be in any segment or sector of industries. But organizations need to understand the method they are adopting or have adopted to survive in the market. One of the areas where management does not give attention to is the procedures, I have seen where correct processes and procedures are not followed and which leads to conflicting requirements and failure of the product result. If the teams and the management are not in sync and do not follow correct procedures or do not communicate the requirements precisely it leads to a conflict of interest, which does not give us the correct output. We cannot have too rigid or too relaxed requirements.

Say, the company is introducing a new product or is enhancing the existing product, the main and important area to keep in mind is the specifications, if the specifications are not defined well then it will affect the production or development of the requirement, technical teams will not be able to understand the real intent behind the end product what is supposed to be delivered and how it will look or what it will do. As I have mentioned earlier, testing is the area where it is missed, and this leads to the errors and failures of the product. It's very important that before any release of the product or enhancement proper testing in various environments is required and has to be mandatory. This area is very robust in the Software industry because unless and until the testing is not done the product will not go into production. Plus, the most important element now is Security, so the security element is required to be included in the testing phase. Feedback loops need to be open and there must be retrospective sessions after every time the product is tested.

So, management is the key to where we need our products to succeed in the market. We need to have robust training and an up-skilling department where the employees can be trained about new products and say new machinery and technologies.

One cannot survive in the market just on basis of introducing cheap and faulty products. A strategic approach to all the above areas has to be kept in mind. Companies cannot survive without knowledge management and technical teams. Management needs to have accurate strategies and procedures to work with the technical teams to introduce fully workable and computable products which can be successful with the customers.

"Make your product easier to buy than your competition, or you will find your customers buying from them, not you." – Mark Cuban

Chapter 24- Parents deserve Respect and Love

We are living in a world where everyone is busy with their life, to survive and be ahead of others. All are in a hurry, be it at work, in business, in politics, sports, everyone is in a rush to beat others and prove to the world that see what I can do or what I am capable of. But, honestly, no one knows why exactly they are on this earth and what is the purpose of their presence, why are they born.

Parents are the most gracious and soothing factor in our lives. They are the ones who raise their children no matter what their situation is, whether financially or otherwise. Bringing a child into this world is not a joke, it needs thinking and agreement between two partners. After a couple of things and looking at their financial position etc., they decide that yes now is the time we can plan for the baby. Once, the baby comes into the world, it's a new world, joy and happiness are what this child brings in their life. And with that new responsibility for raising this little angel. It needs commitment from both parents. This cannot be the responsibility of only either Mum or Dad, both need to commit and understand each other how to raise this child, nurture and cherish this newborn. And yes, the parents do, they will not eat themselves unless and until the baby is not fed. Parents keep track of every step and each move the baby makes, capture that in their memories, and nowadays keep every moment captured in a video. A mother is a gem, she is the one who carries this baby for 09 months in her belly, the pain and agony she goes through the whole time she only knows it, and after giving birth to a child, feeds the baby her milk for close to 03 years. How much love and affection she has for her baby and just cherishes every second this baby of hers is growing. The first smile, the first sound baby makes, the first step a baby takes, and so on damn everything.

In Quran, it mentioned that if one wants to touch the grass of heaven and feel it, they should touch their mother's feet, because under the feet of the mother is heaven. Almighty, also mentioned that if there was no me, then you had to pray and bow down in front of your parents as they would have been your God. So, much respect and elevation are given to the parents by the Almighty, imagine. Parents are one of the blessings of the Almighty, they teach and help us more than any other person in our life, they are always ready to support us through thick and thin, and they feel happy and proud of our achievements. At any stage of life, parents never leave their children alone or helpless. They always protect and guide their children about life, struggles, how to achieve, and how to be the best in the world. They want their children to have the best education. Some parents cannot afford private schooling but to make sure their child gets the best education they cut their expenses to make sure the school fee is paid.

My parents sent me to the best school in our town. It was a missionary school with the best schooling system, with kids studying from rich families, my parents were teachers, teaching in Government schools where the salary is not that good, but they get manageable salaries, despite that, they made my brother and myself study in the best school, I know how they used to cut on monthly expenses and make sure we get best of all. They used to make a monthly budget and stick to that. I know it was sometimes very tough for them, but they used to manage. That's what parents do for their children, and what is then our responsibility, to give our best, make sure we top in our studies, be good and obedient kids, and respect our parents for their sacrifices for us.

It is our responsibility to understand what they have been through and do our best to make them feel proud and make them realize that your efforts are not going down the drain but are worth we will prove that and make you both feel proud. As a child grows and starts understanding the world and society, at the same time he/she needs to understand the value of parents, what they mean, and what level of respect they deserve.

Now, let's talk about parents, we talked about their commitment to their child and how to bring up this kid. Some parents give so much love to their kid, with pampering and making sure whatever stuff the kid asks for is immediately available, etc. I understand that the love for your child is eternal, and no one can question that but there is something called disciple, what is good and what is bad, this also needs to be taught to the children otherwise it may be a problem when a child is in teens and his youth. The first and most important school for a child is at their home, their parents are the first teachers always. Before a kid is sent to school, the education starts far before that in the mother's lap. As a parent, you need to make sure your kid understands:

- What does respect for parents mean?
- How to respect others and gain respect?

- What is discipline?
- When to talk, where, and what?
- What is society?
- How to differentiate between good and bad?
- What is appropriate and inappropriate?
- Teach them the right attitude
- Teach them manners and discipline

And above points are never-ending, you must keep track of a child and watch the patterns, and if any deviations correct them. Bringing a child into this world does not mean a few years of pampering and love and then leaving to school to take care of rest, where one day you find your child is in bad company, and into bad influences, and you don't understand what to do. Do not leave the children at the mercy of society, unless and until you have taught the values you have and want your child to inherit. Sometimes it's too late and your kid is out of your hands, and you are helpless to get it fixed. So, as a parent, there are a lot of responsibilities on you to make sure tomorrow you feel proud of and say he/she is my kid and see what our values are which they exhibit. Parents need to keep in close contact with what is going on at school and know if the child has a problem that needs attention. This requires parents to give up a lot of their free time and for Dads, this means maybe giving up watching football on Sunday or Monday nights because the child needs help with something or say for example math homework or some school project. Kids take a lot of time and patience and then if there is more than one—it sometimes takes both parents to keep up. Kids have interests too and a lot of times it isn't something the parents are interested in, but parents can learn a thing or two along the way too—so it is not wasted time to try to get interested in what they are trying to learn how to do.

Children have multiple needs that must be met by their parents. Children need validation, security, discipline, attention, and affection. If those needs are not met the child ends up with an abandonment wound. The child will be distracted in school because he needs an external focus at all times to avoid the psychological pain he is in. It is impossible to be a good student if you can't even concentrate due to the amount of abandonment pain you are In. Your kids are a gift from God, and you must give them all the love you have. The child complains because he's in the freeze response playing dead in the parent's presence. As parents, we shouldn't want to be feared by our children we should be seen as a safe base, so the child develops a secure attachment. Yelling and hitting your kids is only what humans do, no animal hurts their offspring. In essence, parents' responsibility is to see that children become responsible and capable adults who can pursue their joy and happiness without harming other people. Education (both formal and informal at home) plays an important role here. Children should be able to use their resources efficiently so that they can achieve a higher level of joy and happiness. This does not mean that there should be a narrowing down of their choices. They should be able to do well within their constraints. Parents need to discipline their children but at the same time no need to be pushy and overprotective. Say, if the kid is an average student, don't nag him/her to keep studying well and not letting come out of the schoolbooks and shout, etc. This way your kid gets irritated and frustrated and it makes them more to hate everything around. Rather than support them and make them understand it's okay to be average and that nothing will stop them from doing a lot of things. Parents need to identify what other activities their kid is interested in, say football, singing, painting, etc. help them enhance their passion and you never know if they can be the heroes of their field.

As a parent, unlike what people tend to believe once your children turn eighteen years old and are considered adults in Western countries, they are on their own. Well, let me tell you that as parents of our children regardless of their age, they're still our children and it's a lifelong responsibility to help them, give them advice, and provide them with our home for them in a time of need. We brought them into this world and it's up to us to see that you'll look after them as long as you can and you're alive. That's a PARENT!

Despite, all the areas I talked about and the responsibilities of parents towards their kids, many children do not treat and value their parents in the way they did in their childhood. Arguing restlessly, ignoring due to other life activities, and misbehaving, are the common actions that most of the children of this era do with their parents. When we are young, we are so busy starting our new families, thus in all of this, we do not have time to see that our parents are also getting old, and it is the time when they need our support, love, and care. It is not only unfair to parents but also considered an evil act and sinful deed.

Why are there so many old-age homes around the world? We see that old parents are left in these homes and Children are busy with their lives and families, and not even once realize what these old parents have done for them. How they brought them up, fed, them, gave them the best schooling and education, and made them a person capable of standing on their own feet in the world. Parents deserve the same respect care and love as you deserved when you were a kid. Old parents become the same as when you were children and require support at every step. Our parents need constant health checkups, proper healthy food, clothing, etc. We as children have a big responsibility towards our parents, they have to be respected, taken care of, and given everything they have done for us. Children cannot shed their responsibility because of busy schedules or family or say moving to another country or place. There are scenarios where Children drop their parents at the old age home and abandon them, how sad is it? Also, Children's negligence and not caring attitude drive the old parents to go to old age homes, at least they will get the care and respect they deserve there.

The increase in old age homes in metropolitan cities is not a good development. Over three decades ago, the thought of older parents being sent to old age homes was not easily accepted in India due to the traditional mindset and cultural ethos. The most obvious reason for this trend is the migration of children from their hometowns to metropolitan cities in search of better education, jobs, and improved lifestyles. While the younger generation has no difficulty in moving out of their parental homes and adapting to new lifestyles, the elderly population chooses to remain back due to the attached sentiments of the place. In the Western world, old people are seen standing by the roadside and holding signs that say, "Talk to me for 05min" or "Can you hug me". How sad is this, why are we leaving our loved, adored parents at the mercy of other people? Lucky are those children who have their parents with them and have their blessings. I adored my mum and dad; they taught me a lot and made me a man who is confident and knows what a blessing of parents means. Your blessing of parents is indeed the most precious gift one has. I used to always to my parents, please pray for me, any new thing, or any new journey I was about to take, I used to tell them to pray for my success. Because their prayers are the first which Almighty answers. As I mentioned at the start, Heaven is under your mother's feed and the prayer of your father is a super precious blessing that never goes unanswered, remember this. At the family level, the younger generation should be more thoughtful about the elderly in their homes and should not leave them all alone. In case they need to leave their villages for work, they should take the elderly people with them or should make alternative arrangements so that the eldest family member is not alone at home and does not become a victim of negligence and abuse. The elderly people enjoy the company of their grandchildren, and the kids should not be prevented from mixing with their grandparents. They need regular health checkups and medications. The younger generation must cater to their needs in their last days and should not allow them to go into depression

So, whatever situation you are in, wherever you are settled because of a job etc., never abandon your parents. They deserve your love and affection. As we grow in our life, we also know our parents won't be with us forever, everyone has to taste death at some point in our life journey, so why get involved in a sin where our parents curse us and hate us and cry for us and say why we brought our child to this world who deliberately abandoned us. Never take a curse from parents, because if it happens you will never be successful in life nor will be happy, no matter how much you earn or have a great position. Hurting parents is the biggest sin, a sinful act that the Almighty doesn't like and sends the wrath on those people.

"To lose one parent, Mr. Worthing, may be regarded as a misfortune; to lose both looks like carelessness." — Oscar Wilde, The Importance of Being Earnest

Chapter 25- Mental Health @Workplace

On World Mental Health Day, which is organized by WHO all over the globe on October 10th, I was invited by Amity Institute of Psychology & Allied Sciences (AIPS), Amity University, Noida India as the guest speaker as they were celebrating this day and had organized various Workshops and Seminars.

With me were eminent speakers from various fields like Medicine, Media, Education, etc. So, myself being from the Corporate World was invited to speak on Mental Health at the Workplace. Around 200 students were listening to us and as they are our future Counselors and Psychiatrists, the emphasis was given on, how to fix the issue, how to understand a person who is suffering from a mental health issue, and how to make that person accept the fact that there is no harm in accepting it and fixing it.

We all are aware that in our Corporate we work under a lot of pressure and deadlines hang on us like nuclear bombs. Customers have a lot of expectations and want everything to be delivered within no time, as they are on the other side facing competition from their competitors same as we are facing pressure. So, everyone is running in this hush and rush and wants deliverables to be delivered before even when they say, is it complete?

In this frenzy of activity, both as employees and employers, we find ourselves burning out, not just physically but predominantly mentally. Mental exhaustion has emerged as a significant health concern, manifesting in anxiety, depression, loss of appetite, insomnia, and other related issues. Tragically, individuals are succumbing to despair and even contemplating suicide due to various stressors.

A survey conducted by ASSOCHAM reveals that a staggering 42.5% of corporate employees in India are grappling with depression. Additionally, nearly 38.5% of employees are sleeping less than six hours a day, contributing to a host of health problems including depression, hypertension, and diabetes. Alarmingly, a significant portion of these severe mental health conditions remains untreated, largely because individuals are hesitant to acknowledge their struggles with mental health.

According to the World Health Organization (WHO), the prevalence of depression surged by 18.4% between 2005 and 2015. These statistics underscore the pressing need for greater awareness and acceptance surrounding mental health issues in our society. What is the cause of this all, why do we need 2 – 3 Ambulances on standby outside our offices? I have taken my colleagues to Hospital when they collapsed in Bangalore and I was surprised to see that in the Emergency ward during working hours they see most cases from Corporates, isn't this alarming?

Now, what causes this and according to me the reasons are:

- Friction and unhealthy relationship with your Superiors/Managers
- Not good relationship with our Peers and Colleagues, reason competition and jealousy

- Mixing your Personal and Professional life and not drawing a line between the two
- Very high demand for performance and work pressure
- Majorly, in the present scenario where we have Job Insecurity
- Work-Family conflict is also one factor

We should try to be as positive as we can, our mental health and our thinking power are within us and only we can fix them ourselves. When one thinks Positive and believes in himself/herself and has self-confidence things work accordingly. One needs to set the priority, which means one should know what Time Management is and should manage time very efficiently. After the pandemic the whole norm of work has changed, from the workplace and being at office premises, we now work remotely from home. It was a total shift in how employees and employers were used to interacting with each other. Ever since all changes, everything moved to digital platforms. Interactions, meetings, the team meets, etc., all were carried out on Zoom Webex, Teams, etc. During the start, it was all fine but with time it all started turning hectic and employees started feeling burnt-out and stressed. The productivity suddenly increased because of employees working almost 16 hours or more, the reason for this was there was nothing to do with the outside world as we all were under lockdown, locked inside our rooms and in front of us a laptop and work.

In my example, I was engrossed in the work and worked every day for almost 14-15 hours without a break, because I was eating also in front of a laptop. After a year or so I started feeling stressed and my eyes were strained, I started seeing blurry when I am reading something close like on phone. It was shocking, I never had this issue and see what I did to myself by continuously being in front of a laptop screen, or when not laptop than using the phone. People started having health issues, physical and mental. It was not only work that was stressing employees but being at home there were other issues, being with kids, and parents all the time, along with work, and house chores everything was getting piled up, and yes, no way to get out of this and have my time. Forced to contend with these additional stressors while still having to work, many workers faced unexpected challenges with their mental well-being and needed support while at their jobs. As a result, many employers are now pursuing a renewed focus on employees' mental health for the first time and the mental well-being of their employees. Depression, alcohol, other substance misuse, and anxiety skyrocketed because of COVID. Workers started leaving jobs as they were not able to cope with the unprecedented pressures.

There are tremendous opportunities now, because of COVID-19, where employers need to rethink the workplace and the flexibility that can be provided to employees. Awareness of mental health is the first step. The existing mental health issues in the world are exacerbated by the pandemic and will be further amplified, for many, by the transition back to work. And we saw the impact under "Great Resignations", which was the result of this menace of going back to work. However, we saw how organizations adopted the "Hybrid Model". Under this model, employees are given flexible choices when they want to work from the office and when remotely. This flexibility has given a breather to all workers under a few sectors but not all. Say, manufacturing cannot afford this model for all departments in their company. Now, because of flexibility employees are happy to work a day or two from the office and meet colleagues and friends share ideas, and have their own time. But as I mentioned earlier, the focus needs to be on the mental well-being of a worker. Most important for the workers who can't afford to have this flexible option available.

Apart from the above-mentioned areas, the most important thing for the employees to keep in mind is avoiding competing with others whether at work or anywhere, when you start competing you forget about your ideas and priorities and start running without any goal which turns into mental stress and anxiety. One should compete with itself and set targets when to reach where and track the progress. Most of the time we get caught up in our struggle and make sure the other person does not go ahead and I am left behind. Why, what if the other person is going ahead of you and not you? Be happy for that colleague of yours and set a target for yourself, that this is what I want to achieve. Set realistic targets rather than anything which is not achievable. No one is going to tell you what to do and what not, your manager can give you feedback and guide you in your job or where you need to improve but the rest work has to do itself. Feedback is a good thing and should get now and then, but what matters is whether are you applying the feedback you received in your work and what you do. Are you ready to work on areas where you need attention rather than stressing and overthinking unnecessarily about results and which path to take for achieving them?

The employees who set unrealistic targets and struggle to achieve them are the ones who are left behind. Also, the management should set realistic targets for their workers rather than setting goals that are unrealistic and they know cannot be achieved. If Management knows it's unrealistic then in that case why are you stressing your workers with undue burden, management has to set targets which are achievable and by which workers can bring new ideas and innovations and enjoy working and achieving the milestone. Most of the time mental stress is created by the management of the workers. Managers need to be sensitive about the mental well-being of their employees and make sure they are not burning out their employees. Make sure your employees are not only working but taking breaks, leaves also, and doing other stuff also apart from their regular work. How many managers, talk to their employees one-on-one and try to understand their passions in life? We need to have employee engagement programs; people connect town halls at the workplace where workers can show their talent and feel connected to the organization.

Finally, remember "Your Thoughts are Your Things" and that you think you will get them, so think good, healthy, and positive. Be Optimistic and don't let pessimism come in your way. Make your destiny and nurture it.

Chapter 26- Your Personality

Much discussion surrounds the unique personalities of individuals, whether they be our friends, colleagues, or family members. Indeed, every person possesses a distinct personality, ranging from extroversion to introversion and beyond. Unfortunately, it's not uncommon for people to make judgments about others based solely on their outward demeanor. Such prejudgments are unfair; no one should be evaluated solely on the basis of their personality.

It's important to recognize that initial impressions can be misleading. Someone might appear aloof or abrasive at first glance, but upon getting to know them better, one may discover a wholly different individual beneath the surface. Therefore, it's imperative to refrain from hastily forming opinions about others based solely on superficial observations of their personality.

How many of us know what type of person I am, does an individual know about his real personality or who that person is? There are so many questions that come to mind when one thinks about this subject. Some individuals are not aware of themselves at all, and they come to know about their personality from another person. Most of the time when one faces their analysis of personality, they try to differ or disagree, or they don't want to face their real side as how they look to society or the people in general. People try to hide behind the mask they are wearing. One's personality is flashed in front of the world by the actions and body language and not only what one is saying. When a politician is talking to people see their body language, and that will show how true are to what they are saying, and do they mean what they are promising. So, this means one has to be a very good observer, always.

There are a lot of personality tests on the web, where you answer a few questions and get to know what you are or what type of individual you are, "if you answer them with your gut feeling and are honest", the rest of analysis will do its work and come to conclusion about your persona trait. These tests assess your personality traits and how you think about things and how you react to certain situations. As per Wikipedia, the first personality assessment measures were developed in the 1920s and this was mainly introduced to the armed forces. Since these early efforts, a wide variety of questionnaires have been introduced and developed including the Minnesota Multiphasic Personality Inventory (MMPI), the Sixteen Personality Factor Questionnaire (16PF), and the Comrey Personality Scales (CPS), among many others. Although popular especially among personnel consultants, the Myers–Briggs Type Indicator (MBTI) has numerous psychometric deficiencies. Several instruments based on the Five-Factor of personality have been constructed such as the Revised NEO Personality Inventory. However, the Big Five and related Five Factor Model have been challenged for accounting for less than two-thirds of the known trait variance in the normal personality sphere alone.

I prefer MBTI or Myers-Briggs Type Indicator most, I tried it myself and found that my personality falls under ENTJ-A. You know, it's good to know about your personality and be very much aware of your strengths and weakness. If one works on personality in areas where weakness is on the higher side then it can change his way of life, the way one thinks or works or most important interacts with others. It can boost an individual's confidence and morale and can achieve the best in life. I say you start working on your growth mindset areas by knowing where you fall under, and which persona side. My perception is the perception about myself itself changes from circumstances, situations I face in life (maybe unimaginable tough situations which I came across in life or the easiest situations I came across in life, or can be this way too... a tough situation turned away a piece of cake or the simple one got tougher a big challenge. Tests given in apps, and the web is "not all the way to measure oneself", it's life itself that puts one in various scenarios and how one faces it. Problem-solving attitude may be one to measure, people skills to say for another... I may be good to some people, but others can see the other side of the coin of me. A coin has two sides and can flip itself as per human situations. You may call me good or bad but it's all perception of an individual's brain thought process. Good knowledge about persona testing/measuring apps, but it is up to an individual to ask his conscience to become a better person day by day, instance by instance, person to person, and situation to situation. I am sure you will agree, some things at least, if not, it's again a perception ...it can always differ for everyone.

Now, should we all try these Personality Assessments and see where we are as an individual, I say yes absolutely we should go for it. Should we start putting our Personality Status on our resumes to let the hiring department know about us so that they know what type of person they are hiring, or will give them a fair idea? I think we should put this status or mark it on our CVs like other details and feel proud about it. It will help people to know you more and interact at your intellectual level. Most organizations give the test to the people who apply for jobs with them. Even in most management schools, such tests are used to track the personality trait or say the character of an individual. It helps them to understand the person better and what can that individual bring to the table. How innovative and flexible that person is and will it be a good hire for the company?

Say if I have 20 people in my team, that means I have 20 different personalities to deal with. All will not be the same, and as a manager, I should know how to deal with them and know how to understand their behavior because a lot will depend on that. And if as a manager I know about personalities and have been through various tests related to it, it will help me to be a better supervisor and help my people grow. People always have two areas where they need to focus, skill issues and will issues. These two sides are very important to understand, some individuals don't want to talk about either of them and maybe they feel threatened, which makes them question their credibility or capabilities. But, if they can talk and be open to their issues and discuss them with the person whom they trust or even with the manager, a lot can be solved. It's just that a person needs to identify what is bothering them and what can be done. It all boils down to the personality, maybe the introvert is the factor that is stopping him/her to go forward and talk or insecurity that makes them sit behind.

So, understand your weaknesses and work on them never shy away from sharing with friends or experts and find the solution. Be aware of your personality and be proud of your positive outlook and work on the area where it needs focus and work to be done. It's never too late to work on areas where you feel it's not working. No one is perfect in this world; people are there who are close to perfection and call themselves perfectionists but are not fully perfect. I will say no one should call themselves perfect, we all lack things which as a person I may not be aware of but the other person can figure out. You should be receptive to feedback and criticism; it helps you to grow and correct yourself. People who are defensive and feel attacked if negative feedback is given, are fooling themselves and will never grow, and will remain in their cocoons which is dangerous not only for that individual but somewhere for society.

"People often only see one side to someone's personality, but there are levels." - Ross Lynch

Chapter 27- Life After Lockdown

The world coming to standstill, no one had ever imagined in their lifetime that one-day whole world will be shut down and people locked up in their rooms/houses/condos. Total silence and what was allowed essential services to serve patients and needy ones. The global economy came to a halt. Businesses started struggling as supply and demand were not working at all. Governments were trying to beef up the medical system whether, in developed countries or developing countries, the reason the whole health system was crashing was they were not able to cope with the huge influx of Covid patients.

Angel of death was roaring all over the earth, it felt like God is so angry with humanity that it just wants to end it, and wipe out the people from the surface of the earth. Death was everywhere, people were dying like leaves shedding from the trees in Autumn, what was going on? Our elders, and grandparents started saying that the reason for this catastrophic virus is our sins, people are so engrossed in their materialistic needs, and various inhuman activities that we are seeing this punishment on us from the Almighty. My dad once told me while watching the news and seeing the crisis all over and the deaths, "dying in the present scenario is like, dying the death of a stray dog whom no one wants to touch", and it was true, patients dying in hospitals were sealed in the plastic bags and taken away to the far away graveyards, the loved ones of that poor fellow were not allowed to touch or see the body, how unfortunate. No one knew who is next and how can we save ourselves from this deadly virus.

However, in this chaos and catastrophe, one good thing happened and that was our mother earth started breathing healthy, and the overall climatic condition started improving drastically. For example, the most polluted countries started seeing clean fresh air and climate improvement. The carbon-dioxide footprint started reducing, and the best part our ozone layer started healing. Scientists have confirmed that air quality in certain regions has improved during the pandemic period. As industries, aviation, and other means of transportation stopped, air pollution drastically reduced in countries severely affected by the virus, such as China, Italy, and Spain. A reduction in commuting due to work-from-home policies has also played its part in reducing carbon emissions. The response to this health crisis will shape how people will deal with a climate crisis in the next decades. Times of change can lead to the introduction of long-lasting sustainable habits. Thanks to the outbreak, some habits that are incidentally beneficial to the environment may last since people will have experienced scarcity. For example, the reduction of travel, personal consumption, and food waste. People have started realizing what is more important to them, what needs to be kept, and what is not.

After 02 years of chaos and things subsiding, the virus turned into a sort of endemic and people got used to new norms like wearing masks and making sure they keep away from crowds is working. Now, we all are excited to be out of our dens and visit our favorite cafes, meet friends, be at work with colleagues, and have that sip of morning coffee with them. Sounds exciting, but I want to say something which I feel is important for all, that is, ask yourself "What is Important for me?". Yes, before you get engrossed in your daily routine life think about what is important for your life, is it my family, my health, my kids, my job, or what matters to me? Doing the retrospect of importance and then stepping out of your house and starting a new life. Because when you know what is important to you, then only you will take proper precautions and be mindful about how to keep yourself safe because if you won't, I am sure not today but someday you will be infected as no one is safe, the infection is airborne and very much present in the environment. A comprehensive new survey of the effects of the pandemic on the atmosphere, using satellite data from NASA and other international space agencies, revealed some unexpected findings. The study also offered insights into addressing the dual threats of climate warming and air pollution.

Things have changed, the way we used to live before the pandemic has dramatically changed. Pandemics taught us a new way of life, a new norm. Earlier we used to be so much in hurry and running like manic after materialistic things. We were busy with work, planning vacations, planning new houses and cars, and whatnot. But that all has stopped, people realized that they need to stop taking a break and do some thinking. As I mentioned earlier, what is important to survive, and where should I invest more time? It became important to think about your health, have a healthy lifestyle, and make sure you have good immunity to fight such kinds of viruses. Because during the pandemic we saw people with high and healthy immunity fight the virus and survived if they were infected by Covid. Also, a lot of loopholes or cracks surfaced in people, it showed how much we all are vulnerable and stressed. It made us think that how important is the family and being with them. There were pros and cons both on the relationship side, some relationships became stronger and some failed, basically couples and married people. As individuals started being with each other 24/7, it showed how much they want each other and need to be together.

Mental health, this area became more prevalent, mainly because people started working remotely from home and there was no way to be out or go to the office. The mental stress increased dramatically in working people as they not only had to deal with the work but also the house chores and dealing with the kids. Because of COVID-19, where employers need to rethink the workplace and the flexibility that can be provided to employees. Awareness of mental health is the first step. The existing mental health issues in the world are exacerbated by the pandemic and will be further amplified, for many, by the transition back to work. And we saw the impact under "Great Resignations", which was the result of this menace of going back to work. However, we saw how organizations adopted the "Hybrid Model". Under this model, employees are given flexible choices when they want to work from the office and when remotely. This flexibility has given a breather to all workers under a few sectors but not all. Say, manufacturing cannot afford this model for all departments in their company. Now, because of flexibility employees are happy to work a day or two from the office and meet colleagues and friends share ideas, and have their own time. But as I mentioned earlier, the focus needs to be on the mental well-being of a worker. People have started coming back to the offices, as the companies have adopted the hybrid model, but still lot of workers are adamant to join back and are comfortable working remotely. As an employer, they don't need to push the workers to be at the workplace but rather give them options, this will avoid unnecessary mental stress for an individual.

Because of mental stress, depression, and anxiety during the pandemic period, there were a lot of suicides as workers either lost their job because the company was not able to sustain themselves during the period or because of unexpected work pressure. So, we all need to be cautious about the mental health of our workers, and also it is the responsibility of an individual to take help in case of depression, anxiety, and stressful situation. Keeping things inside you and unnecessary overthinking is not going to help or solve the situation. One needs to take control of his actions and work on them with confidence and wherever required talk to parents, friends, or the experts.

All countries have opened and avoided any sort of Lockdown and let the economy get started with the opening of businesses and industries with the realization that we cannot just sit locked forever as this invisible enemy is going to be with us for long and we must start adapting to new changes and a new way of life. Businesses have seen tremendous losses and the major impact was on small and medium-sized companies. Governments tried their best to support businesses financially be at any sector. Because of the new rules and new norms companies have to adapt to new rules, say now when companies are calling their employees back to work, they have to make sure their facilities are properly sanitized every time, their masks are distributed to workers, and enough social distancing factors are kept in place. So, there is a lot of change in how companies used to operate earlier and how they have to adapt now. We saw a lot of industries come to a halt in a pandemic, mainly Airlines, Tourism, Retail, etc. Now after the opening of the lockdown and restarting of the economy, these sectors are trying to make some gains. The airline industry is doing well, however, the tourism industry is still struggling to make an impact as still, people around the globe are hesitant to go on long vacations. Now, there is the overhead cost of masks, PPE kits, hand sanitizers, etc. in these sectors, which has increased the cost, and people are not ready to shell out money as all are trying to save because the market situation has become so volatile.

Now, people are taking a calculated risk, they know things are not good. The economy all over the globe is dangling and there are risks of a recession on the horizon. Everyone wants to have some sort of saving so that they can survive, feed their families, and have health coverage. As the economy is not doing good and companies are struggling to survive, there is more risk of people that are losing their jobs, which is happening to some extent. When there are so many risk factors, how can one think of going on tours and vacations, unless you are rich and have millions and millions saved? The poor and middle-class people I am sure cannot afford travel and vacation at all. One more thing which has happened due to the pandemic is poor has become poorer and the rich have turned richer. This wide gap opened the fishers in a society where there is so much inequality all around the world. Everyone is worried about their survival and moneymakers are making enough to have their bank balances rising, without giving any heed to the poor population and their well-being. There are at least four ways the COVID-19 pandemic has increased inequality:

- Higher-paid workers are working from home while lower-paid blue-collar workers typically do not have this option, say workers working for manufacturing plants.
- The major share of low-paid workers are in essential services such as nursing, policing, teaching, cleaning,

refuse removal, and store attendants where they are more likely to come into contact with infected people. So, a lot of poor and below-middle class people end up in hospitals and die

- Lower-paid workers are more represented in the sectors that have suspended activities such as hotels, restaurants, and tourism services which I mentioned earlier were mostly affected by a pandemic
- Lastly, the pandemic is increasing poverty and inequality between richer countries that can afford to bail out their firms and provide social safety nets, and poorer countries that cannot do so.

The pandemic turned into a big windfall for the ultra-rich. The staggering rise in the stock market is a testament to this. In the US, over 44 million people lost their jobs and unemployment surged to 15% between April and June 2020. Yet the fortunes of the top five billionaires rose by $102 billion, increasing their wealth by 26%. The combined wealth of US billionaires increased by over $637 billion to a total of $3.6 trillion, which is considerably more than the entire wealth of the 54 countries on the African continent. Some of the biggest winners are those with high stakes in the technology sector. Digital retail vendors, conferencing platforms, and social media groups have reaped the benefit from the lockdown and the shift to remote work. So, we know who these companies were, like Zoom, Webex, MSTEAMS, FB, Twitter, etc. people started using these platforms to be connected to their loved ones, friends, and colleagues. Dating apps boomed because that was the only way to date strangers as one cannot go to a bar or café. So, the revenue of these techs. companies started rising high. Companies moved all their meetings, conferences, training, etc. to an online format. All schools, colleges, and universities around the world turned to remote online classes. Everything started happening online, now need to travel for meetings onsite, when you can do it online. Now, you can see how these companies make money.

So, there are pros and cons of this pandemic on a larger scale, be it the economy, mental health, relationships, businesses, and so on, all learned lessons about life and survival. We as the people understood that the world is one giant place where all are connected no matter what, we are not separate living in different regions, it's one. If one gets affected rest of the world gets affected, this is the major lesson this Covid-19 pandemic taught us and the world leaders. Because of the pandemic, we realized how badly we have damaged the earth's climate and overall balance; the impact is huge. If still, we don't understand the whole situation then I don't know what will save us or will happen to the earth. The impact of climatic change is so evident that we are seeing unprecedented rises in temperatures across the globe, floods, earthquakes, wildfires, etc.

Be safe and stay alert for your family, kids, and people who care for you. Most important for yourself, because if you are Infected everything you have around will be affected. THINK....!

Chapter 28- My Poems after Lockdown

As the lockdown lifted, a new dawn emerged, breathing fresh life into weary souls. People savored the simple joys of freedom, rediscovering the profound meaning of life itself. Stepping out beneath the open sky, strolling along familiar streets, each moment felt imbued with newfound significance in the wake of the pandemic.

What does freedom truly signify? Is it the sensation of being under the vast expanse of the heavens, embracing a revitalized existence? And what does it mean to survive a perilous virus, emerging resilient in the face of adversity?

In the midst of this reawakening, I found myself inspired to capture these sentiments in verse. For in moments of happiness or sorrow, poetry has a way of surfacing from the depths of the heart, giving voice to the emotions that stir within. Thus, I embarked on a journey of crafting poems, weaving together words that resonated with the essence of our shared experiences.

Some of these verses now grace the conclusion of my chapters, serving as reflections on the lessons gleaned from the pandemic and our collective evolution. As we move forward, it is essential to ponder these lessons and consider how we may apply them in shaping a brighter future for ourselves and generations to come.

Mother Earth is Breathing

Now, see mother earth is breathing,
Now, see birds and trees are breathing,
All the destruction is caused by us,
All chaos and disruption are caused by us.
We the humans are culprits of every mess around,
We need to correct our actions and stop this mess.

If we ignore the damage caused,
What is the use of us being locked?

Now, we need to be awake and aware,
Now, we need to think and realize,
To take care of mother earth,
Who feeds us and cares for us.

Let's pledge to stop cutting trees,
And let them grow to give us life.
Let's pledge to stop trading plastic,
And let the ocean and fishes be ecstatic.

If our mother earth breathes right,
So will be all breathe right,
And if our mother earth is not living right,
So, will we not live and flourish, right?

And, if we deny and disrespect mother earth,
Then the day is not far from us, a doomsday for sure.
Alas, see what we got, a virus which locked us all,
And see what we see, mother earth is breathing,
Everything in nature is smiling and feeling fresh.

Thank You, Almighty

Here is my gratitude, a thank you to the Almighty,
For making me such a wonderful person all the way,
A person that enjoys 'every day,
A person who shows care and compassion,
Will, it is enough to thank you Almighty,
For this gift every day whenever I pray?

Here is my gratitude, a thank you to the Almighty,
For my sweetest parents,
Who makes me always feel so happy.. always feel so high?
Who shows me so much love that can make me fly?
Parents who always really trust me,
And now I will never let them down,
Thank you, Almighty... It is never enough to thank you
Till forever... to thank you till I die

Here is my gratitude, a thank you to the Almighty,
For sending me someone so very real,
Someone that treats me so right,
that knows how to deal and heal,
I've always dreamed of someone caring
For my deep wounds to tenderly heal.

How could I thank you Almighty?
How could I prove that I'm so very grateful?
For giving me such a lovely person that made all my life so beautiful
That lovely person that I appreciate
Is YOU... my love and I appreciate your presence.

Here is my gratitude, a thank you to the Almighty,
For giving me confidence, courage, and passion,
For making me a person to care and think of others,
I am grateful to you for listening to me when I need you,
Always by my side, in my heart and soul,
Saying, do good, see good and hear good 'because I am with you.

Embrace Humanity

Why do we see hate everywhere?
Why do we see empty states everywhere?
Don't you think that life is getting hard?
To live and survive with all this chaos?

Why is everyone on the throat of another one,
People are killed & others are tasting the nectar of wine,
Why some are making merry of war,
People are killed because of crazy war.

Humanity cannot bare the changes,
Of the world's temperamental stages,
We can't believe the darkness in everyone's heart
I guess they should be all blocked and caught.

Don't you think that life is more than hate?
Don't you think we should get away before it's too late,
People are too greedy they never get enough!
So, let's embrace humanity and let crooks go to hell.

Where are your feelings people... why are you so cold?
We all want to live in peace, peace for the world,
When will you throw the sword?
Sword of hate and venom,
Let's turn this venom into pure love.

Don't you ever feel shame?
But it's not the time to blame as its lame,
It's time to get together... as we are one and not enemies,

Let’s live like brothers and sisters, let’s embrace humanity,
Let all the world come together as one big family,
Let’s make this world a better place,
Let’s make the peace and tranquility.